"I think I think..."

VINTAGE SERMONS BY

Reuben Welch

f·

THE FOUNDRY
PUBLISHING®

Copyright © 2024 by Reuben Welch
The Foundry Publishing®
PO Box 419527
Kansas City, MO 64141

978-0-8341-4316-6

Printed in the
United States of America

Cover design: Brandon Hill
Interior design: Sharon Page

Library of Congress Cataloging-in-Publication Data
A complete catalog record for this book is available from the Library of Congress.

Most Scripture references are from the *Revised Standard Version* (RSV) of the Bible, copyright 1946, 1952, 1971 by the Division of Christian Education of the National Council of the Churches of Christ in the USA. Used by permission.

All other Scripture references are from the King James Version (KJV), which is in the public domain.

The internet addresses, email addresses, and phone numbers in this book are accurate at the time of publication. They are provided as a resource. The Foundry Publishing does not endorse them or vouch for their content or permanence.

10 9 8 7 6 5 4 3 2

Contents

Foreword
I Think I Think

Really? We're publishing a book of sermons originally preached thirty to fifty years ago? Yep! And if you take the time to read them, you will know why!

Some books, essays, and sermons are tied to a particular time and place. Others transcend the time and space of their original context. The sermons preached by Reuben Welch included in this volume are both. They certainly were relevant to the time and place of their delivery, but I think you will discover many timeless truths in these insightful pages.

Reuben Welch became chaplain of Pasadena College (now Point Loma Nazarene University) when I was a student there in 1968. The days were electric. The Vietnam War was raging, social heroes like JFK, RFK, and MLK had recently been martyred, college students across the country were protesting, and hippies were challenging social norms. At the same time, there was a spiritual revolution with the advent of Jesus People and the Asbury revival that was sweeping the country.

Reuben Welch took center stage as our college chaplain in the middle of those times. He was an engaging speaker with a great sense of humor. But, much more than that, he was a New Testament scholar who knew how to speak words of wisdom and truth to an auditorium full of radicalized college students. For many of us—I daresay most of us—he became one of the most influential people in our lives. For those of us going into pastoral ministry, he was our model of what good preaching could be. For those of us who simply needed counsel from someone over the age of thirty whom we could trust, he was the listener who showed us what it meant to care for others. We all wanted to be like Reuben!

Reuben's influence was not limited to the college community. He was in demand as a speaker and preacher at other college campuses, pastors' conferences, camp meetings, lay events, and pastors-and-spouses retreats across the country. Many of the older, established generation didn't quite know how to respond to him since he didn't fit the mold of a traveling evangelist. He preached the Word in ways no one had really heard before. There was no one quite like Reuben Welch. He had the unique gift of being able to mine the depths of Scripture and invite us into an exploration of the wonders of the Word in ways that were new, refreshing, insightful, and worth remembering. His messages were pure gold.

Fast-forward fifty years, and Reuben's influence continues to be evident in the preaching, thinking, and living of so many of us who sat under his ministry in those years. I still remember many of the sermons I heard him preach fifty years ago—not because they were catchy or cute but because in those sermons there were nuggets of truth that were key to my understanding of the gospel and what it means to be a follower of Jesus Christ. And I am not alone. There are hundreds of people like me who have been deeply impacted by Reuben's life and ministry.

Reuben is so loved and admired that many of us still remember not only the profound nature of his teaching but also some of his idiosyncrasies. We call them "Reubenisms." They are warm reminders of his down-to-earth style and homespun wisdom—perhaps something he inherited from his grandfather, "Uncle Buddy" Robinson, a well-known country preacher of the early twentieth century.

I'd like to share a few Reubenisms. In a Q&A session, when asked a tough question, Reuben might begin with the phrase that titles this volume: "I *think* I think. . . ." Or he might say, "I can hardly wait to hear what I have to say about that!" After saying something he wanted to emphasize or thought was especially important, he might say, "That's so good I have a notion to get saved all over again!" Or when he was poking fun at some of the foolish theological notions of the day, he might say something like, "God can forgive sin, but what can he do with stupidity?" His humor often rang true to our everyday lives—for instance, "Don't try to be holy when your children are young!"

This volume comprises two parts. In the first part, Reuben's daughter, Susan Welch Armstrong, has transcribed and formatted ten of Reuben's previously unpublished sermons. One might say these are ten of his best, but that would not do justice to the dozens of others that were just as important. These ten are offered as a sample of the preaching that helped shape a generation of students, pastors, and ordinary followers of Jesus. The second part is a reprint of the book *To Timothy and All Other Disciples: Probing Thoughts from Second Timothy.* These six sermons were preached to 2,500 high school students from around the globe at the Nazarene World Youth Conference held at Estes Park, Colorado, in 1978.

I encourage you to take your time as you read. Listen carefully to how the Spirit of God might be speaking to you through Reuben's messages, preached decades ago. I am confident you will find not only words of wisdom in these messages but also words of truth, life, and hope!

Ron Benefiel
Director of the Center for Pastoral Leadership, Point Loma Nazarene University
Former President, Nazarene Theological Seminary

Foreword
To Timothy and All Other Disciples

As I sat on the ground at the foot of the Rocky Mountains with more than two thousand other teens from across the world, I became absorbed in and mesmerized by what I heard and saw. Even as a sixteen-year-old youth, I recognized I would never be the same again because of this experience. I realized that something unique was occurring. My vision of Christian Scripture was becoming refocused; my understanding of reading the Bible was undergoing transformation. It was as if the man who was speaking each morning was inviting us to a whole other reality as he challenged us to engage in Scripture in ways I had never imagined possible.

This international youth conference had gathered to explore Christian discipleship. Each day's schedule included small groups, large discipleship training sessions, recreation, evening worship, and special music features. However, the morning time slot from 8:40–9:15 forever changed my life. The daily program listed this session simply as "2 Timothy Bible Study by Reuben Welch." Each morning, all 2500 of us gathered in an open field with the snow-capped Rockies in the background. At the center of the field was a large, flat-topped rock no more than three feet high and twelve feet wide. This rock served as the platform upon which the next half hour would take place for five days. From the first day onward, that platform became known as Reuben's Rock. In the first introduction of our Bible study leader, we were given his full name: Reuben Welch. However, for the rest of the week, he went by simply Reuben.

More than four decades later, I still vividly recall that first morning. As Reuben began to read from 2 Timothy 1, it was as if the very rhythm of his voice was setting the stage for a dance that was about to begin. While the biblical text served as the lead in this dance, Reuben was the faithful partner. As I watched him and heard the words that came out of his mouth, it was apparent that the Bible was not merely the object of his study or the source of his sermon—it was his passion, his love, his friend. It was plain to see he had been engaged in every step of the dance with this partner for days and weeks, months and years. He had listened to it, learned from it, asked questions of it, agonized and wrestled with it. In his journey from listening to wrestling, it seemed he had entered into a vibrant, childlike joy that sparked not only his own imagination but now also overflowed into the imaginations of all of us who witnessed this dance with Scripture. It was as if he desired for *his* friend to become *our* friend! Somehow, he was inviting us to join him in listening to the text ourselves—to learn from it, to ask questions of it, even to agonize and wrestle with it.

With quiet tears, Reuben spoke as if he now had become Paul saying to his spiritual Timothys gathered around Reuben's Rock, "I am grateful to God . . . when I remember you constantly in my prayers night and day" (2 Timothy 1:3). I had never seen anything like this phenomenon before. I did not even realize it was happening, but suddenly 2500 of us were being invited by Reuben (or was it Paul?) to join him and participate in the dance with Scripture.

As he continued, with references to recalling Timothy's sincere faith that first lived in Timothy's grandmother Lois and his mother, Eunice, it was as if Reuben were speaking not only of Timothy's faith but also of *our* faith; not only of Timothy's mother and grandmother but of our own mothers and grandmothers. Paul's challenge to Timothy had become Reuben's challenge to us: "Fan into flame the gift of God that is within you" (v. 6). I had never begun to imagine that this reality could happen with the Bible, but it had: the world of Paul and Timothy had so collided with the world of Reuben that now Reuben was inviting us to join that collision so that Paul and Timothy, Eunice and Lois, Reuben, and all of us were dancing in such a way that this ancient text was alive and breathing. Rather than simply applying the biblical text to our lives, Reuben was inviting us to join him as he joyfully entered the dance with Scripture! By the Holy Spirit, through this servant of God named Reuben, ancient text and contemporary audience had beautifully and authentically become one.

In the pages that follow, the message of Paul to Timothy and "all other disciples," as Reuben Welch faithfully presented that message more than forty-five years ago, is as engaging and formative now as it was then. The biblical content of this material is profound, and the writing style is beautiful. Indeed, Reuben's authentic engagement with Scripture is mesmerizing and highly contagious. It was for me then; it is for me now. It continues to be a gift to the church.

As I listened to Reuben those mornings, that sixteen-year-old guy began to imagine, *Wow! What a beautiful way to give your life to the next generation: dancing with sacred Scripture in such a way that others desire to join that dance. I think that I want to do that when I grow up.* He never realized then, but from that moment to this very day, Reuben Welch has served in my own Christian journey and ministry as one of the Lord's most significant mentors in my life. I have turned to him for wisdom at the most significant junctures of my journey. I have discovered that Reuben Welch not only *preached* well about Timothy's mentor named Paul, but he also *lived* that mentorship well. His preaching was embodied in his life. Thank you, Reuben, not only for faithfully dancing with Scripture but also for inviting us to join you in that dance. Your fingerprints are beautifully etched upon more of our lives than you could ever imagine.

Timothy Green
Professor of Old Testament Literature and Biblical Theology
Dean of the Millard Reed School of Theology and Christian Ministry
Trevecca Nazarene University

Preface

"I think I think . . ." is a phrase that's always been associated with my dad, almost as much as "We really do need each other." It captures the marvelous tension he maintained between what he was sure about and what he was still considering. That openness to new ideas, a tentativeness about non-essentials, is one of the qualities that endeared him to so many.

Preparing this collection of my dad's sermons has been a joyful journey. I have been blessed over and over as I've listened to numerous cassette recordings of him preaching, some from as early as 1968. At ninety-nine years of age, his voice is so much weaker now; getting to hear him in his prime has been a poignant treat. I have chosen ten of my favorite sermons to include in this volume, all previously unpublished.

He is known for his sermon series, but the majority of those I've included were standalone messages. The last three are exceptions; they were part of the revival series on Romans preached at Point Loma College (now Point Loma Nazarene University) in the fall of 1980.

Not every message he preached was recorded, so my choices were limited to those he had saved over the years (collected on more than two hundred tapes). I looked for several that were not among his collection: the chapel message on using our "fifteen minuteses," "The Gospel in the Carols," and "When Life Doesn't Go in a Straight Line" are three I would love to have included.

I have done my best to help the reader hear him as you read. He yelled a lot, so I didn't put all of his yelling in caps, but here and there the all-caps treatment denotes a LOUD word or phrase. Words or phrases with special emphasis are in **bold**. He often paused between words in an important phrase: Those. Have. A. Period. After. Each. Word. He had a tendency to quickly rattle off lists of phrases. I have used the indented format of his earlier books for many of these lists to help the reader see them clearly. His asides are *italicized*, but what I didn't include were his chuckles and laughter at his own jokes, of which there were many. I didn't know how to indicate the times when his voice cracked as he began to get emotional—which he always did, at one time or another, in every sermon I ever heard him preach. Too bad his gestures can't be preserved, except in our memories.

As I listened to these tapes over many months, several things stuck out to me. The life of my older sister, Pamela Ann, had a tremendous effect on him and his preaching. She was born with brain damage in 1949, when he and my mother, Mary Jo, were pastoring in Hawaii before it was a state. At the age of twelve, when we were living in Pasadena, Pam had to be institutionalized, and she was in some kind of care facility until she died at age forty-four. There was no silver lining to that situation, and one of his missions was to refute, in no uncertain terms, any notion or teaching that everything happens for a reason or that God brings something good out of every tragedy.

Of course, living and serving in a college community and counseling with hundreds of students over the years gave him a deep desire to assure the doubter, comfort the hopeless, and remind those whose faith was weak that Jesus comes all the way down to where we are with love, grace, mercy, and strength for the journey.

I think his ministry was affected by various religious movements of the time that watered down or distorted the gospel, like the prosperity gospel and the "expect a miracle" craze. His sermons also responded to the Jesus Movement of the late sixties and early seventies. I recall some overzealous, super-spiritual students (some who even challenged his teaching) who had perhaps become so heavenly-minded—well, you know. One of the sermons is titled "Ordinary Life," and that was a theme for him—bringing Jesus and our Christian life down out of the clouds and into the ordinary business of day-to-day living.

One of his most important missions was to illuminate the character of God as seen in Jesus. He often said, "A false *mental* image of God is as bad as a false *metal* image." Another pattern was to help his listeners see the arc of God's purposes throughout history, which culminated in "the best thing God ever did" when God sent Jesus. I'm sure his years of teaching Old Testament contributed to that; you'll hear it over and over again in these sermons.

He always gave a warm greeting to the congregation but rarely, if ever, had an introduction or opening story, like most preachers do today. He almost always began with his text. His sermons contain copious amounts of Scripture—much, but not all, of which he quoted from memory. Most of the Scripture in these sermons is from the Revised Standard Version (which he thought was the best), but some of the longer passages, which he had memorized years before, were from the King James Version, particularly Hebrews 11 and the Christmas story in Luke 2.

He never apologized for reading a lot of Scripture. For one thing, he read it (or quoted it) so beautifully and with such marvelous expression that we were enthralled; for another, he truly believed that whatever he read was better than anything he was going to say. He loved the Word and taught us love it too.

I sincerely hope these sermons are the blessing to you that they have been to me. They are still as relevant, moving, probing, challenging, and encouraging as they were when they were first preached.

A couple of final notes. For the ten transcribed sermons, I have added a short paragraph to the beginning of each one to add context about where, when, or under what circumstances the sermon was preached. Finally, the planning committee for this book would like to thank Rev. Tom Crider for his vision, input, and generous support in making this project a reality.

Susan Welch Armstrong
Pastor of Care and Discipleship
Reynoldsburg Church of the Nazarene

Sermon #1
Faithing
Hebrews 11–12:2 KJV

This is a combination of three sermons; he titled these, "Faithing," "What the Saints have to say about Faith," and "When You Run Out of Fantastic, Persevere." This sermon wasn't included in the book When You Run Out of Fantastic . . . Persevere *but was honed over several years of "marinating" in Hebrews. He always quoted this passage in full, from memory, in the King James Version.*

[1] Now faith is the substance of things hoped for, the evidence of things not seen.
[2] For by it the elders obtained a good report.
[3] Through faith we understand that the worlds were framed by the word of God, so that things which are seen were not made of things which do appear.
[4] By faith Abel offered unto God a more excellent sacrifice than Cain, by which he obtained witness that he was righteous, God testifying of his gifts: and by it he being dead yet speaketh.

⁵ By faith Enoch was translated that he should not see death; and was not found, because God had translated him: for before his translation he had this testimony, that he pleased God.
⁶ But without faith it is impossible to please him: for he that cometh to God must believe that he is, and that he is a rewarder of them that diligently seek him.
⁷ By faith Noah, being warned of God of things not seen as yet, moved with fear, prepared an ark to the saving of his house; by the which he condemned the world, and became heir of the righteousness which is by faith.
⁸ By faith Abraham, when he was called to go out into a place which he should after receive for an inheritance, obeyed; and he went out, not knowing whither he went.
⁹ By faith he sojourned in the land of promise, as in a strange country, dwelling in tabernacles with Isaac and Jacob, the heirs with him of the same promise:
¹⁰ For he looked for a city which hath foundations, whose builder and maker is God.
¹¹ Through faith also Sara herself received strength to conceive seed, and was delivered of a child when she was past age, because she judged him faithful who had promised.
¹² Therefore sprang there even of one, and him as good as dead, so many as the stars of the sky in multitude, and as the sand which is by the sea shore innumerable.
¹³ These all died in faith, not having received the promises, but having seen them afar off, and were persuaded of them, and embraced them, and confessed that they were strangers and pilgrims on the earth.
¹⁴ For they that say such things declare plainly that they seek a country.

¹⁵ And truly, if they had been mindful of that country from whence they came out, they might have had opportunity to have returned.

¹⁶ But now they desire a better country, that is, an heavenly: wherefore God is not ashamed to be called their God: for he hath prepared for them a city.

¹⁷ By faith Abraham, when he was tried, offered up Isaac: and he that had received the promises offered up his only begotten son,

¹⁸ Of whom it was said, That in Isaac shall thy seed be called:

¹⁹ Accounting that God was able to raise him up, even from the dead; from whence also he received him in a figure.

²⁰ By faith Isaac blessed Jacob and Esau concerning things to come.

²¹ By faith Jacob, when he was a dying, blessed both the sons of Joseph; and worshipped, leaning upon the top of his staff.

²² By faith Joseph, when he died, made mention of the departing of the children of Israel; and gave commandment concerning his bones.

²³ By faith Moses, when he was born, was hid three months of his parents, because they saw he was a proper child; and they were not afraid of the king's commandment.

²⁴ By faith Moses, when he was come to years, refused to be called the son of Pharaoh's daughter;

²⁵ Choosing rather to suffer affliction with the people of God, than to enjoy the pleasures of sin for a season;

²⁶ Esteeming the reproach of Christ greater riches than the treasures in Egypt: for he had respect unto the recompence of the reward.

²⁷ By faith he forsook Egypt, not fearing the wrath of the king: for he endured, as seeing him who is invisible.

²⁸ Through faith he kept the Passover, and the sprinkling of blood, lest he that destroyed the firstborn should touch them.

²⁹ By faith they passed through the Red sea as by dry land: which the Egyptians assaying to do were drowned.

³⁰ By faith the walls of Jericho fell down, after they were compassed about seven days.

³¹ By faith the harlot Rahab perished not with them that believed not, when she had received the spies with peace.

³² And what shall I more say? for the time would fail me to tell of Gedeon, and of Barak, and of Samson, and of Jephthae; of David also, and Samuel, and of the prophets:

³³ Who through faith subdued kingdoms, wrought righteousness, obtained promises, stopped the mouths of lions.

³⁴ Quenched the violence of fire, escaped the edge of the sword, out of weakness were made strong, waxed valiant in fight, turned to flight the armies of the aliens.

³⁵ Women received their dead raised to life again: and others were tortured, not accepting deliverance; that they might obtain a better resurrection:

³⁶ And others had trial of cruel mockings and scourgings, yea, moreover of bonds and imprisonment:

³⁷ They were stoned, they were sawn asunder, were tempted, were slain with the sword: they wandered about in sheepskins and goatskins; being destitute, afflicted, tormented;

³⁸ (Of whom the world was not worthy:) they wandered in deserts, and in mountains, and in dens and caves of the earth.

³⁹ And these all, having obtained a good report through faith, received not the promise:

⁴⁰ God having provided some better thing for us, that they without us should not be made perfect.

12Wherefore seeing we also are compassed about with so great a cloud of witnesses, let us lay aside every weight, and the sin which doth so easily beset us, and let us run with patience the race that is set before us,

² Looking unto Jesus the author and finisher of our faith; who for the joy that was set before him endured the cross, despising the shame, and is set down at the right hand of the throne of God.

(Hebrews 11:1-12:2)

Amen!

When I was young and heard this last portion about the great cloud of witnesses, I had a mental image of the battlements of heaven, whatever they are. *I don't know what they are, but don't you love the word?* And the saints looking over. You know, I think a better image is the arena, and those who have run the race before us are in the stands, all around, and they've run their race, and now we are running ours.

It's interesting, "Wherefore seeing we also are compassed about with so great a cloud of witnesses, let **us** lay aside every weight, and the sin which doth so easily beset **us**, and let **us** run with patience the race that is set before **us**."

There's a shift in the center of gravity here, isn't there? So, they have run theirs and now we are running ours, the writer says, surrounded by a great cloud of witnesses. Well, amen!

You got anybody in that crowd? I imagine you do, and so do I. But I've come to understand that these persons are not witnesses in the sense that they are onlookers; they are not spectators, they are witnesses in the sense that they testify. They are called to the witness stand to bear witness. The word behind that is the word "martyr," those who were ultimately killed because they made their confession.

A couple of questions, or three or four, are going around in my head at the same time. That is, I wonder how we think about faith. How do we perceive it? What does it mean to be a believer? What does it mean to have faith? And I'm wanting to know, what is it that these witnesses are shouting out to us?

The first thing that I hear from them, what they shout out to us is faith is not just something you **have**, faith is something you **do**! Let's take a minute and go back through that great chapter. And as we do, I want us to notice the great words of action.

> By faith Abel **offered...**
> By faith Enoch was translated, *but if you go back to Genesis 5, Enoch* **walked with God.**
> By faith Noah **built...**
> By faith Abraham **obeyed** and he **went out...***Do you hear those words?* not knowing whither he went,
> By faith he **sojourned** in the Land of Promise, dwelling in tabernacles with Isaac and Jacob...
> For he **looked** for a city that hath foundations whose building and maker was God.
> By faith Abraham—*I love the way the thing is put together*—by faith Abraham when he was called, **obeyed...**
> By faith Abraham, when he was tried, **offered** up Isaac: and he that had received the promises offered up his only begotten son...

By faith Isaac **blessed** Jacob and Esau... *You know, Isaac didn't really do very much but you've got to give him credit, he kept the blessing going! Amen!*

By faith Sarah **received strength** to conceive seed....

These. All. Died. In. Faith.

You know what they did? They saw the promise out there, they were persuaded of it, *I love the progression,*

> they saw it,
>> they were persuaded,
>>> they embraced it, and
>>>> they made their confession. Praise God!
>>> And they walked,
>> and they looked,
> and they chose,

and they took their path in light of the great vision.

And Joseph looked off into the future and gave commandment concerning his bones, *that's a great line!* You know, we don't often think about it but all through the Exodus, across the sea, into the desert, through the struggles in the wilderness, on the Sinai, back around, and then finally into the Land of Canaan... Do you know that everywhere those Israelites went, somebody had to carry the bag of bones? "What you got there?" "Well, I got these bones, see." "Whose bones?" "Well Joseph's!"

Everywhere they went they carried with them the luggage that bore witness to the faithfulness of God to bring them out and bring them in and Joseph said, "It's coming!" We are here because of the faith and vision of those who have gone before, and we can't SEE it but we carry about with us the blessed baggage of those who believed and trusted before us! They

> ...**subdued** kingdoms, **wrought** righteousness, **obtained promises**, **stopped** the mouths of lions, **quenched** the violence of fire, **escaped** the edge of the sword, out of weakness **were made strong**, **waxed valiant** in fight, **turned to flight** the armies of the aliens....

What kind of faith is this? Do you see how it functions and how it works? I mean, we're talking FAITH! How did it express itself?

These people say to us that faith is not just something you **HAVE**; it's something you **DO**!

It's how you walk,
 how you offer,
  how you build,
   what you choose,
    what you esteem,
     what you value,
      how you sojourn!

You know what impresses me? Hardly any of this went on in church! That's weird! I mean, where does faith belong? Well, it belongs in church, especially on Sunday morning. And we sing together,

"O for a faith that will not shrink though pressed by every foe
That will not tremble on the brink of any earthly woe."

O for a Thousand Tongues to Sing
Words: Charles Wesley
Music: Carl Glaser, arr. by Lowell Mason

And the organ is beautiful and the words are great and we get the warm, sentimental feeling and there's none of it here! In fact, hardly any of this is religious! Strange!

You know what I hear, faith isn't just something you have
 it's how you offer,
  how you walk,
   it's how you build,
    it's how you respond to what you hear from God,
 it is how you behave when God contradicts God,
  It's how you look on and bless the children and send them
  out. It's how
you respond to the demonic demands of the king
 and how you refuse,
  and how you choose,
   and esteem,
  what things you value,
 how you make your choices in harmony with what you
 believe,
how you walk and live your life,
THAT'S what faith is!

Does that make any sense? Does that compute?

I'm thinking that faith needs a verbal form. It needs to be put into an action word and the best thing I can come up with is what I think is a participle. Faith needs to be teased a little bit into something active like **"faithing."** Will that be alright? Well, let's run it by…

"Noah, what in the world are you doing pounding pegs into that monstrosity in your back yard? Rain?! It never rains! What are you doing?" "I'm faithing!"

"Oh Abraham, looks like you're leaving the good life behind! Where are you going, everybody else seems to be coming?" "Well, I heard this voice..." "Where are you going?" "I'm not real sure." "What are you doing?" "I'm faithing, just faithing."

"Moses, where are you going?" *I can just hear him,* "I'm off to see the Pharoah, the terrible Pharoah of Egypt!" "Why are you doing this?" "Well, there was this bush that burned, see, and I heard a word." "Whatcha doin', Moses?" "I'm faithing, I'm faithing."

There's Jeremiah down there in the pit. "What are you doing, Jeremiah?" "I'm faaiitthhiinngg!"

"What about you, Hosea? I heard your marriage broke up and your wife took off for the bright lights. Whatcha doin', Hosea?" "I'm faithing, I'm faithing."

"Habakkuk, how about you? What I hear these days is that there aren't any blossoms and there aren't grapes and there aren't any olives, and the herds are gone and the stalls are vacant. Whatcha doin' Habakkuk?" "I'm faithing!"

"You pilgrims wandering in dens and caves, in sheepskins and goatskins, destitute, afflicted, tormented!" *Don't you love the parenthesis, (of whom. the world. was. not. worthy).* "What keeps you GOING?" "We're faithing!"

I'm about to decide I like that word!

"Oh Jesus, what are you doing hanging on that cross between two thieves?" Can you hear him? "I'm faithing, I'm faithing!"

You see, it's not just something we **have**; it isn't something we carry around with us. But It. Is. Something. We. **DO**. Amen!

Well, what about us?

> We're making our choices,
>> making our decisions,
>>> walking our walk,
>>>> offering our offerings,
>>>>> making our sacrifices, but mostly,
>>>>>> we are living and working and
>>>>>>> walking and doing...

That's faithing, isn't it?

Well, actually, I hear another word from these saints. You know what I hear them say? "It pays to hang on!" I'm sure there is a more theological way to say that, but the only other theological term I can come up with is, **"Don't quit!"**

You remember that poster from years ago, that cat hanging on at the bottom of the rope that said, "Hang in there, baby!"? *Wonder if that cat's still hanging there?*

Faith really means endurance in hope. Oh, there are a couple of lines in here that are just staggering to me. Do you remember the line that begins,

> Through faith also Sara herself received strength to conceive seed, and was delivered of a child when she was past age, because she judged him faithful who had promised. Therefore sprang there even of one, and him as good as dead, so many as the stars of the sky in multitude, and as the sand which is by the

sea shore innumerable. These all died in faith, *listen to this*, Not.
Having. Received. the Promises.

Did you hear that?

They saw them afar off, they were persuaded of them, and embraced
them, they made their confession. What was it?

    They were out of sync with the world,

        strangers and pilgrims,

            another set of values,

                another drum rhythm,

                    another posture,

                        another world view.

Then you remember, when it comes down to "What shall I more
say, for the time would fail me to tell of...." You know, he just gets
on a roll. And there were those that subdued kingdoms and wrought
righteousness and great and wondrous things happened and then
right in the middle of verse 35, *they should at least put another verse there,*

> [35]...and others were tortured, not accepting deliverance; that
> they might obtain a better resurrection: [36] And others had trial
> of cruel mockings and scourgings, yea, moreover of bonds and
> imprisonment: [37] They were stoned, they were sawn asunder,
> were tempted, were slain with the sword: they wandered
> about in sheepskins and goatskins; being destitute, afflicted,
> tormented; [38] (Of whom the world was not worthy)...

Miracle, miracle, miracle, victory, victory, victory...and others
were tortured, "yea moreover," *says the King James*, "bonds and
imprisonment," and the WORLD. WAS. NOT. WORTHY! They

wandered in deserts and mountains and dens and caves of the earth!
And these all,

 the victories and the un-victories,

  the defeats and hurts and sorrows,

   persecutions,

   triumphs and the victories and the joys,

these all having obtained a good report through faith Received.
NOT. The. Promise!

Folks, these people have something to say to us, don't they? In the
verses before Chapter 11 it says, you have need of confidence so that
you don't give up your faith. We have need of PATIENCE to see the
END of our faith. But I tell you, men like Abraham and Moses and
the prophets,

they heard a voice,

 and they started the journey,

  and they threw their lives away for their hopes and their
  dreams and their goals,

   and they were crushed down and steamrollered
   in the end but…

THEY NEVER GAVE UP!

And my crazy mind pictures that when the steamroller passed over
them, those "Gumbys" got up and pushed themselves back into
shape and kept on going. And God said, "I am not ashamed to be
called their God!" Don't you know that when the promise finally did
come, they were mighty glad they hadn't quit? Amen!

That's AWESOME to me! They threw their lives away and they
never saw the fulfillment of their dreams. They died before the

promise came, but thank God the promise came! And they are saying to us, "DON'T QUIT! Don't throw away your confidence!"

Do you have faith? "Oh yes, I have faith!" And I want to say, "do you?" What do we mean?

    Do we just praise God?

        Are we just so aware of his precious presence?

            Do we just believe everything's going to come out alright?

            Do we just feel so close to Jesus?

            Oh sure, we have faith!

And then I read the chapter and say, "Do we really?" How about the way we walk? Is there a straight line between how we feel and how we live? Is there any connection between the sentiment, the emotion and

                what you choose and

            how you build and

         what you refuse and

      how you endure,

     the things you hope for,

   the things you dream for,

the things you ultimately give your life to?

And then I'm talking to some of you who are saying, "Don't talk about faith to me, I don't have any faith!" I'm talking to some of you who've got problems, are carrying heavy burdens, and some of you can only see the dark side of everything. And you're saying, "I don't have any faith!" And yet, *are you listening?* You're putting one foot in front of the other, making your choices, walking the walk. And sometimes you don't have any feelings, but you still "esteem the reproach of Christ greater than the riches of Egypt." When it comes right down to it,

> you keep on walking,
>> you keep on offering,
>>> keep on choosing,
>>>> and keep on enduring. Well, amen!

My old granddad would say, "Are you a'catchin' on?"

I think I think that when it comes right down to it, what really matters is that we **Just Don't Quit!**

You know, folks like us who aren't real young anymore, we know what it means to hurt and to fail. We don't have a lot of shining ideals anymore. But you know what really matters when it comes right down to it? **Just Don't Quit!** Amen!

Maybe what really matters is not that we have all the miracles and feel all the feelings, but finally we just keep looking to Jesus, the author and the finisher of our faith who for the joy that was set before him, kept on going. Amen! And so, he is saying to us, "Come on, come on."

I wonder if I'm talking to anybody who's got half a notion to quit. Jesus is our example, he is our pioneer, he's walked the way before us, and he's saying to us, "Just keep comin'." Amen! "Just keep comin'." And I'm talking to people who know

> heartache,
>> sorrow,
>>> loss,
>>>> failure,
>>>>> hurt, and

victory, and

triumph, and

miracle.

And here we are. And the word of God is. Our faith is really about, how we walk and how we build and how we esteem, and finally, that we **Just Don't Quit!** Amen!

Well, what about us? We're on this side, and, thank God, we know that the promise has been fulfilled, so we have a different kind of vision, yet in some ways we don't. We too, live by faith, and we know that the promise has come, but the promise has not been consummated, so, in that sense, we and they and they and we are all a part of the great movement of God toward the future. And so, we live in hope, we walk by faith and not by sight, but we've got two great things going for us. We've got the word of these saints who say to us, "Don't forget, what really matters is

how you walk and

how you offer and

how you choose and

what you esteem,

how you endure,

how you keep on hoping,

how you don't give up!" Amen!

Does that make sense?

But the promise is real, hallelujah! So then, while we run the race, with these words in our ears, we are looking to Jesus, the author and the finisher of our faith who for the joy that was set before him endured the cross, despising the shame. And don't you know, Jesus was glad he DID. NOT. QUIT!

So, what's their word for us? I think their final word for us is **Don't quit!** Amen! The promise is real, and while we walk in the midst of the mystery, in the joy and in the sorrow, there are these marvelous witnesses who say to us, "Really, faith may not be what you do in church as much as it is

> how you build and
>> how you choose,
>>> how you esteem,
>>>> how you carry on your life,
>>> how you endure and
>> work and
> how you evaluate things in line with the purposes of God."

And I say, praise God!

"God Leads Us Along"
Words and Music: G.A. Young

"All the Way My Savior Leads Me"
Words: Fanny Crosby
Music: Robert Lowry

Sermon #2
He Did Not Have to Survive
Philippians 2:4–10 and Various

He preached this sermon quite a bit, and it is one of the most remembered and impactful of all his sermons. It was preached in church settings and college settings; I heard him preach it at a faculty retreat in the late '80s. It was a prophetic message to those institutions that were intent on survival, sometimes at too great a cost. This version (with a few adjustments from other versions) was preached at Portland First Church of the Nazarene.

I'd like to have you open up your Bibles to Philippians chapter 2, and I'd like to read a portion of that marvelous passage of Scripture.

And I want to talk about what I'm going to talk about, and I don't want to talk about it. And I have to say before I talk about it, that it is a passage through which God has been talking to my heart.

Let's begin reading in verse 4 of chapter 2 of the book of Philippians.

> [4] Let each of you look not only to his own interests, but also to the interests of others. [5] Have this mind among yourselves, which is yours in Christ Jesus, [6] who, though he was in the

form of God, did not count equality with God a thing to
be grasped, [7] but emptied himself, taking the form of a
servant, being born in the likeness of men. [8] And being found
in human form he humbled himself and became obedient unto
death, even death on a cross. [9] Therefore God has highly exalted
him and given him the name which is above every name, [10] that
at the name of Jesus every knee should bow, in heaven and on
earth and under the earth, [11] and every tongue confess that Jesus
Christ is Lord, to the glory of God the Father.

Oh my! Isn't that a great passage?

Now would you turn over to a passage in the book of John, chapter
10, beginning at verse 11. I have read to you some words about Jesus
from Paul, and now I would like to read to you some words of Jesus
about himself.

[11] I am the good shepherd. The good shepherd lays down his
life for the sheep. [12] He who is a hireling and not a shepherd,
whose own the sheep are not, sees the wolf coming and leaves
the sheep and flees; and the wolf snatches them and scatters
them. [13] He flees because he is a hireling and cares nothing for
the sheep. [14] I am the good shepherd; I know my own and my
own know me, [15] as the Father knows me and I know the Father;
and I lay down my life for the sheep. [16] And I have other sheep,
that are not of this fold; I must bring them also, and they will
heed my voice. So there shall be one flock, one shepherd. [17] For
this reason the Father loves me, because I lay down my life,
that I may take it again. [18] No one takes it from me, but I lay
it down of my own accord. I have power to lay it down, and I
have power to take it again; this charge I have received from my
Father."

I want to talk to you today on the matter of **survival**. *I wish I had a better word. If you can think of a better word when we're done, I want to hear it.* But for lack of a better one, it is **the matter of survival**.

As I read the stories in the Gospels, I find myself in awe of the
    freedom and
        authority and
            integrity and
                power of Jesus.

The older I get and the more I'm privileged to teach the Gospels, the more profoundly I'm impressed by the
    freedom and the
        authority and the
            integrity and the
                power of Jesus.

I have come to believe that the foundation of these attributes was the fact that he had faced and settled the Issue. Of. Survival. **He did not have to survive!** Therefore, he was free to live his life in obedience, and out of that obedience came his incredible
    freedom and
        authority and
            integrity and
                power.

And I've already repeated those words too much and that lets you know that they are words that I want for myself and that I want to experience in the fellowship of believers.

Having settled the issue of survival, Jesus experienced incredible freedom to **obey** his Father without compromise and to **be** what he was supposed to be.

It's going to take a while to tell you what I'm going to tell you, but I've already told you what I'm going to tell you!

Let me run that by again. Jesus settled the issue of **survival**. He. Did. Not. Have. To. Survive, and having settled that issue, he was incredibly free to be obedient to his father without compromise.

Do you remember at his temptation? He had experienced the mighty presence of God his Father in the waters of the Jordan. The heavens were opened, the Spirit descended, the voice of the Father was heard, "You are my beloved son in whom I am well-pleased."

I believe that Jesus left the waters of Jordan in the awareness that he was the Son of God, the Messiah, anointed of the Holy Spirit, and the task to which his Father had called him was the task of suffering servanthood. Now, whenever in his life that knowledge came to him, by this time, it was clear.

But he wasn't ready yet. And the Spirit drove him into the wilderness where he was tempted 40 days and 40 nights without food. And the understatement is, "and afterward he was hungry."

We know just about how long someone can live who's on a fast, somewhere around 50, 55, maybe 60 days, don't know. Jesus fasted 40 days and 40 nights and was tempted. Everything in him was crying out for SURVIVAL.

He knew himself to be the Son of God, the Messiah; he knew he'd been anointed of the Holy Spirit. But here he was in the wilderness about to STARVE to death.

Folks, do NOT, repeat, do NOT begin your ministry by starving to death! People will not beat a path to your bones! *I think we'd have general agreement on that, don't you think?* That is not the way to start your ministry!

Here is Jesus, he knows who he is, he's ready to begin, and he's starving to death in the wilderness. And Satan comes to him and says, "Turn these stones into bread." And he could have done it, but he had settled the issue!

Do you know how he responded? He responded with a word from Deuteronomy 8 in which his Father said to the children of Israel,

> ² And you shall remember all the way which the LORD your God has led you these forty years in the wilderness…. ³ And he humbled you and let you hunger and fed you with manna…that he might make you know that man does not live by bread alone, but that man lives by everything that proceeds out of the mouth of the LORD.

Did you hear that? Jesus had settled the issue of survival. HE. DID. NOT. HAVE. TO. SURVIVE! That is an awesome thing to me! Can you see that? He knows who he is,
    he's full grown,
        full blown,
            ready to go,
                anointed of the Holy Spirit.
            The seal of the Father is upon him,

the power of God is in him,
and he's starving to death in the wilderness and his answer to
the supplying of his needs is "NO!" HE DID NOT HAVE TO
SURVIVE; therefore, he was totally free to obey. Hallelujah!

Let's go into his ministry a little bit. There's a whole new direction
in the life of Jesus beginning in chapter 5 in John's Gospel after the
healing of the man by the Pool of Bethesda. Beginning there and
running on through the Gospel of John there are some astounding
passages of Scripture in which Jesus denies himself. Listen to
these; some time you just need to read through the Gospel of John
beginning in chapter 5 and see what Jesus says about himself.

> 5:19a Truly, truly, I say to you, the Son can do nothing of his
> own accord, but only what he sees the Father doing....
> 5:30 I can do nothing on my own authority; as I hear, I judge;
> and my judgment is just, because I seek not my own will but the
> will of him who sent me.
> 5:41 I do not receive glory from men.
> 6:38 For I came down from heaven, not to do my own will, but
> the will of him that sent me.
> 7:16 My teaching is not mine, but his who sent me.
> 7:28b But I have not come of my own accord; he who sent me is
> true....
> 8:28b I do nothing on my own authority but speak thus as the
> Father taught me.
> 12:49 I have not spoken on my own authority; the Father who
> sent me has himself given me commandment what to say and
> what to speak.
> 14:10b The words that I say to you I do not speak on my own
> authority; but the Father who dwells in me does his works.

Folks that's an awesome pile of Scriptures,
not MY words,
    not MY authority,
        not ME,
           not MINE,
               not MY power,
                   not MY judgment,
                       the Father, the Father, the FATHER!
And the people said, "No man ever spoke like this man!" "Who
is this that the winds and the waves obey him?" "Who is this that
controls the demons and heals the sick and raises the dead?!"

Not I, not I, not I, not I. I tell you; Jesus did NOT have to survive,
and having settled that issue, he was FREE to do his Father's will.

Oh, how in heaven's name is Jesus able to maintain his sense of poise
and his sense of peace and his sense of direction in the midst of all
the conflicting powers and influences and currents of thought present
in the first century?

Do not think that Jesus just lived in a quiet, peaceful, rural setting!
Palestine in the 1st century was alive with all kinds of conflicting
thoughts and ideologies and desires.

There were the conservative Sadducees: "rich republican
Episcopalians," working within the system, and they were after Jesus.

There were the Pharisees: the "moral majority," law and order, and
they were after Jesus.

There were the Zealots: left-wing radicals, who were ready to overthrow the government. To say nothing of the withdrawn Essene commune. And here is Jesus. How does he keep his direction?

He is pushed,
    he is pulled,
        he is driven,
            they grab ahold of his clothes,
                they want to grab ahold of his mind,
                    they want to grab ahold of his
                    AUTHORITY!

How in heaven's name does he keep his head screwed on straight when he hardly has time to eat or sleep? I'll tell you how, he settled an issue, he did NOT have to SURVIVE; therefore, he could obey. Oh, I praise God for that!

At his trial he said, "I came to bear witness to the truth." It's as though he were saying, "I am committed to the truth. If I live, I live. If I die, I die!" He didn't have to save himself; he did NOT have to SURVIVE!

And because he'd settled the issue of survival, he was able to live in the midst of all the conflicting pressures. He was able to keep his head on straight and his vision true because he settled the fundamental issue of survival.

And I am overwhelmed by his
    freedom and his
        integrity, his
            authority and his
                power.

For that matter, think with me a minute about Saint Paul. How did he keep his own direction straight? You want to talk about a complex situation! You have the Hellenistic religions,

> the Greek religions,
>> the Roman religion,
>>> the political powers, you have
>>>> Paul raised in a Jewish ghetto in a gentile world,
>>> you have a man who is a Jew to the core and is
>> called to the gentile world who has to interpret the gospel

and everywhere he goes there is STRESS, there is PRESSURE, from his own people and from outside. How's he going to keep it all straight?

Somewhere along the way he said, "For to me to live is Christ..." (Phil 1:21), "If we live, we live to the Lord, and if we die, we die to the Lord; so then, whether we live or whether we die, we are the Lord's" (Rom. 14:8). And then in Galatians 2:20 "I have been crucified with Christ; it is no longer I who live, but Christ who lives in me; and the life I now live in the flesh I live by faith in the Son of God, who loved me and gave himself for me."

SOMEWHERE along the way he had settled the issue of SURVIVAL. And because he did not have to SURVIVE, the energies, the creativities of his life were not directed toward survival, they were directed toward OBEDIENCE. Therefore, he had incredible LIBERTY, incredible AUTHORITY. He was able to **come** and to **go** and to **be** because preserving himself was not the issue. Obedience to God was the FUNDAMENTAL issue of his life.

And I guess I'm yelling loud enough for you to understand that I think that is the fundamental issue for us, too!

Well, you know very well where I'm going with this…have you settled that fundamental issue? *Just thought I'd throw that in as I move toward the altar call. So, get ready.*

I think everybody faces this somewhere along the way and responds to it one way or another.

One of my favorite stories is about when Ahaz was king of Judah. *You'll have to forgive me for being an OT teacher for all these 23 years or so, OK?* When Ahaz was the king of Judah in the time of Isaiah the prophet, Pekah was king of Samaria in Israel, and Rezin was king of Damascus in Syria, and over here was Tiglath Pileser, the king of Assyria.

And Assyria was beginning a westward move. *In theological, historical language, the big bug is going to eat the little bugs.* And the big bug starts coming this way and he's going to eat this bug and this bug and so the little bugs say, "If we stick together, maybe we can stand him off!"

So Pekah and Rezin form a coalition and they say, "We need to go down and get Ahaz to help us, and if we all get together, we can fight him off." And in the words of the old hymn, Ahaz says, "Please, Mr. Custer, I don't want to go!" *Do you sing that hymn in your church? It's in the back of the hymnal somewhere.*

And Ahaz is trembling like a leaf, it's found in Isaiah chapter 7. He and all the people of Jerusalem are just trembling like a leaf because these two guys, Pekah and Rezin, are going to come down and make Ahaz do what he doesn't want to do, and if he doesn't, they'll replace him with their own man.

And then God speaks to Isaiah the prophet, and says, "Take your son, Shear-Jashub…" *How's that for a name?* "You go to Ahaz, take Shear-Jashub and…" *I love this line*: "You go meet Ahaz at the end of the conduit of the upper pool on the highway to the Fuller's Field, *right there by the green house,* and you say to him, 'Ahaz, trust God, have faith, stand firm. You don't have to worry, these two kings are like smoldering stumps, and they're going to burn out. You can trust your security to God!'"

But Ahaz couldn't do it. Instead, he goes over and makes a deal with Tiglath Pileser the king of Assyria and gives him offerings and pledges him obedience and brings Judah under Assyrian bondage in an awful period that lasts for more than 200 years…because he had to **survive**. And Judah was never the same, but they survived.

I'll be saying this to you again before we're done…If we have to survive, we will. Yes. Ahaz did, he could, and he did.

Let's go into the New Testament. You remember King Herod? You remember when John Baptist was preaching, and he condemned Herod and then Herod put John in prison, and Salome danced? And the King made the rash statement, "Ask what you will, I'll do it." And Salome said, "Give me the head of John the Baptist." And Herod was not happy, but in the presence of his guests and nobles he had to save face, and he did. He had to survive, and he did, and took the head of John Baptist. But he survived.

And I think about the rich young ruler; Jesus said to him, "Go sell what you have and give to the poor and come and follow me." But he said, "I've got to survive!" And he did, he survived. And he went away sorrowful because his great possessions had him, but he survived.

Do you remember at the arrest and trial of Jesus, Annas and Caiaphas were saying, "It is expedient that somebody die! If not, we are going to lose our place and our nation!" We have got to SURVIVE! And survive they did. And Pilate washed his hands and he survived. And Jesus went off to die outside the city gates between two thieves. He said, "I came to bear witness to the truth," and he Did. Not. Have. To. SURVIVE!

And Jesus is the one with freedom and
> integrity and
>> authority and
>>> power!

Well, draw a line under that. Let's talk about ourselves for a minute, but let's be safe for a little bit.

Let me talk to you for a minute about our nation. I do not speak as a political analyst, I do not speak as a military strategist, or one who has studied deeply the affairs of war and peace. I am just one of the citizens who has some thoughts way down deep inside. I've come to believe something—if our nation has to survive, it will. In the midst of all that's going on, if we have to survive, we can, we will.

In the process we may
> denude the mountains,
>> gobble up our resources,
>>> drain the bowels of the earth,
>>>> pollute the rivers and the seas,
>>>>> darken the skies,
>>>>>> peel off the green hills,
>>>>>>> do what we need to do,
>>>>>>>> we can survive.

And we can drain off our brain power and turn it into destruction and channel our creativity into the building of monstrous engines of war, but we will survive.

Way down inside my little simplistic heart, *allow me that*, I have this feeling, what if, what if, we did **not** have to survive.

Let's assume for a minute that we do not have to survive as a nation. All we have to do is to be righteous,
>to establish justice,
>to ensure domestic tranquility,
>to provide the blessings of life and liberty to ourselves and our posterity,
>to let justice roll down like waters and righteousness like a mighty stream.

What if all we had to do was to cancel the order for a couple of missiles and feed the starving for ten years. What if that's all we had to do?

What if we could channel the incredible brain power of our country toward

the beautifying of the land,
the creation of jobs,
the education of our children
the alleviation of poverty,
to restore the beauty,
the goodness,
the wonder of our land?

But everyone knows we have to SURVIVE! *And I vote yes on that, of course.* And we probably will.

I'm thinking simplistically, I know. I'm not making a political statement about what we ought to do, I'm saying what if, what if we didn't have to? And all of our incredible marvelous resources could, in fact, be channeled to justice and righteousness and peace.

Something in me rises up to that.

Let's come a little closer to home…but let's still be safe.

If our Nazarene colleges, if my college, Point Loma College, has to survive, it will. We can adjust the curriculum, we can adjust the entrance requirements, we can open up the admissions policies, we can do whatever we need to do.

If we have to survive, we can survive, we're good at it. We can work with tuition, we can work with grants, we can cater to the dudes with mega bucks, to do what we need to do to survive, if we have to survive. We can shift our trustees, we can shift our accountability, we can do whatever we need to do to survive.

Now whether or not we are a Christian college, a liberal arts college committed to who we are is a moot point, if the issue is survival. And if the issue is survival, we can survive…and we will pay the price.

Good evangelicals that we are, we are consummate pragmatists. There isn't anything that works that we do not know how to sanctify and make it "meet for the master's use." We're good at that, you know. Whatever works is obviously under the blessing of God! And when a super church gets superer, what do we do? We take the leaders of it and run them around the country and say, "This is the way to do it." Obviously, it's the will of God because it works!

We are good at that! **We can survive**! But oh my, sometimes, way down in my innards I get this feeling… What if we didn't have to survive? What if we could settle that issue once and for all and say, we do **not** have to survive?

What we have to do is to obey God, as best we know, about what it means to be a Christian liberal arts college. And God knows that's a razor's edge, a hard line to walk

> to be Christian liberal arts,
>> to bow down to the lordship of Jesus,
>>> to learn what it means to teach and to care,
>>>> to liberally educate the people God has given us.
>>>>> To be the kind of people in the school we
>>>>> believe God wants us to be,
>>>> where justice is present,
>>> where equity is present, and
>> where we do not have to compromise in order to exist,
> *which everybody knows we do.*

And I love that place and have spent the last quarter of a century there, oh my! *I bet if I grew a beard, it'd be gray!*

I tell you what I believe with all of my heart. We. Do. NOT. Have. To. Survive! But if we settle that issue, we suddenly are aware of incredible freedom to be uniquely what we believe God wants us to be as a Christian liberal arts college!

Truth is, I believe the same thing about the Church of the Nazarene. We do NOT have to survive!

Now, if we have to survive, oh we will, God bless us all, we know how to survive. We know how to adjust apportionments, we know how to reorganize our top structure, *we do it every so often; we'll probably do it again next General Assembly.* We can do what needs to be done in order to survive; we can rally the troops and support the programs.

Now, if being the people we believe God called us out to be is a moot point, a debatable item, an issue up for grabs… If SURVIVAL is the fundamental issue, then other issues come under that and are open for editing. But if we could ever settle the issue of survival, then we will experience an INCREDIBLE FREEDOM to be what God wants us to be.

If we live we live, if we die we die, but we begin to experience
> FREEDOM and
>> INTEGRITY and
>>> AUTHORITY and
>>>> POWER.

You're not going to like the way I'm going…I'm coming down. Is that OK?

Let's talk about this, Church—you do **not** have to survive. If you have to survive, you will, you will, you are survivors. You already know that.

If you have to survive, you will.
> You can adjust whatever needs to be adjusted
>> you can do whatever needs to be done
>>> you can cater to whoever needs to be catered to
>>>> you can go with whatever flow you need to go with
>>>>> in order to survive.

Now whether or not you are the people God intends you to be is not the issue if the issue is survival. Does that compute?

You know, this church doesn't even have to survive. There's only one thing you have to do, and that is to be obedient and responsive to the will of God, to the love of God, to be the people of God.

I don't know if I ought to tell you this but, *you probably already know it,* but if this church would be obliterated off the face of the map...you'd make the *Herald of Holiness*...in December.

It takes time to process this stuff, you know. I always like to read about the people who just got married 'cause I just met their children!

Let's talk about ourselves. I think I'll just testify for a minute...*I'd rather talk about you.* Truth is, I don't have to survive. If I have to, I can.

>I can go with the flow,
>>I can make the compromises,
>>>I can work with the system,
>>>>I can do what I need to do,
>>>>>I can get by.

That's the old American way, you know, get by. It's the pioneer spirit. You can get by, you can make it, you can survive, you can do whatever you need to do.

But, if you don't have to survive you can
>love without getting back,
>>you can give without receiving,
>>>you can serve without have to grow from it,
>>>>you can do the work of God without running it

through the cost effectiveness computer!

If you don't have to survive you can
lend without having to get it back,
you can scratch somebody's back and they don't have
to scratch yours,
it isn't dog-eat-dog anymore,
it isn't business as business anymore!

If we don't have to SURVIVE, we are FREE, we're FREE!

Don't you wish it was as simple as that?

A couple of things that I believe profoundly...*can't tell you how deeply I believe this*, if the issue is not **survival** but **obedience**, we will survive, we will more than survive, we will **triumph**, hallelujah!

But we aren't off the hook.

I know, and so do you, the subtle temptation to make the shift from obedience and freedom to the matter of survival.

I believe that if we obey, we will be more than conquerors. I also know that if the issue becomes survival, oh, we will survive, but we are left with
the erosion of our integrity,
the slow binding of our freedom,
the diminishing of our authority, and
the loss of power.

How many directions do we want to go with this? Want to talk about you and your business? If you have to survive, brother, you will,

> you can cut the corners,
> you can do what you have to do,
> you can pay the price,
> you can do whatever it takes to survive.

And in this dog-eat-dog world, the way times are now, you can survive. Whether what you have at the end is in fact what you want, is not really the issue.

But if you can ever settle it, you do **not** have to survive. Oh,

> the **freedom**
> the **authority**
> the **integrity** and
> the **power**!

The other thing is this, everybody knows, and so do I, and so does God, that we live in a fallen world, and we have to survive. And I know and so do you, if our Christian colleges are going to make it, they've got to do some things they'd rather not do...to win games, to attract students, to make ends meet. They can't do everything they want to do because they've got to survive.

You can't do everything you want to do in the world of business. There's some things you don't like but you've got to do them because you have to survive. Of course, I know that, you know that, and God have mercy on us all, it's kind of the way it is in this world. And after all, a man's got to live, I know that!

But way down inside, aren't you glad that one day, one man came into this world

who faced the situation of compromise,
who faced his own crying desires,
who faced the crying desires of those around him,
who faced all the political ramifications of his
ministry,
but he DIDN'T have to survive. And he lived his life in UTTER OBEDIENCE and TOTAL LOVE and TOTAL RESPONSE to his Father, **And. He. Did. Not. SURVIVE!**

He went all the way to death and then his Father RAISED him from the dead and ENTHRONED him at his right hand. Folks,

> [6]...though he was in the form of God, did not count equality with God a thing to be grasped, [7] but emptied himself, taking the form of a servant, being born in the likeness of men. [8] And being found in human form he humbled himself and became obedient unto death, even death on a cross. [9] Therefore God has highly exalted him and bestowed on him the name which is above every name, [10] that at the name of Jesus Every. Knee. Should. Bow.
> (Phil. 2:6-10)

And I think about that, and the petty little compromises, and the little corners we cut, and the radical shifting that sometimes takes place away from ministry to survival. And in the process, the very things for which we live, we **destroy** because the issue becomes **survival**.

You can see why I don't want to talk about this. I wish we could live at a simplistic level. Seems to me when it finally comes down to it, there isn't any other way to live than in a spirit of repentance that exposes our lives with all of our petty compromises, all our fundamental will to survival, to the healing, loving, grace of God.

I thought about it this way…What if, *I think I believe this*, what if the fundamental will to survive, which is basically my will to control my own destiny, is the original sin? I think I think that our will to survive must bow to the **sovereignty** of Jesus.

I can't go on talking all morning, *well I can but I ain't a gonna, it's just going to seem like it!*

Somehow our will to survive must come to the cross of Jesus so that our

> exaltation,
>> our life,
>>> our destiny,
>>>> our being,
>>>>> our fulfillment,

is not in our own control but surrendered to his sovereignty.

Somewhere it's got to be, if I perish, I perish. **Survival** is not the issue; the issue is **obedience**.

Would you bow your heads with me?

Hear these words from hymn #144:
"When I survey the wondrous cross on which the prince of glory died
My richest gain I count but loss and poor contempt on all my pride."

When I Survey the Wondrous Cross
Words: Isaac Watts
Music: Lowell Mason

I'm talking to some of you for whom the issue of your life has been survival and so you pay **this** price, and **this** price, and **this** price, in order to survive.

Will you think with me like this? What if you didn't have to survive? If that could ever be settled, then you could have

> the freedom to love,
> the freedom to give,
> the freedom to obey,
> the freedom to be.

I want for my life

> the **freedom**
> the **integrity**
> the **authority** and
> the **power** that Jesus had.

And I believe it's related to the issue of **survival**.

If you want to come and pray while we sing, I wish you'd do it.

Sermon #3
How Do God's People Get Ready for God's Good Thing?
Luke 3:2b–17 and
Various Scriptures from the Gospel of Luke

This sermon was preached on a Sunday morning at Pasadena First Nazarene in 1972, not too long after the Pasadena College community was informed that they would be leaving Pasadena and moving to Point Loma in San Diego. Just that summer he had completed a commentary on Luke as part of the Beacon Bible Commentaries. The college community and the church community were all reeling with the news of the move; Dad was reeling. And out of that chaotic time came this wonderful word focusing on the message of John the Baptist from the Gospel of Luke. Note: He always referred to him as "John Baptist."

Pastor Earl Lee read the following Scripture:

> [2] . . . The word of God came to John the son of Zechari'ah in the wilderness; [3] and he went into all the region about the Jordan, preaching a baptism of repentance for the forgiveness of sins. [4] As it is written in the book of the words of Isaiah the prophet,

"The voice of one crying in the wilderness:
Prepare the way of the Lord,
make his paths straight.
⁵ Every valley shall be filled,
and every mountain and hill shall be brought low,
and the crooked shall be made straight,
and the rough ways shall be made smooth;
⁶ and all flesh shall see the salvation of God."

⁷ He said therefore to the multitudes that came out to be baptized by him, "You brood of vipers! Who warned you to flee from the wrath to come? ⁸ Bear fruits that befit repentance, and do not begin to say to yourselves, 'We have Abraham as our father'; for I tell you, God is able from these stones to raise up children to Abraham. ⁹ Even now the axe is laid to the root of the trees; every tree therefore that does not bear good fruit is cut down and thrown into the fire."

¹⁰ And the multitudes asked him, "What then shall we do?" ¹¹ And he answered them, "He who has two coats, let him share with him who has none; and he who has food, let him do likewise." ¹² Tax collectors also came to be baptized, and said to him, "Teacher, what shall we do?" ¹³ And he said to them, "Collect no more than is appointed you." ¹⁴ Soldiers also asked him, "And we, what shall we do?" And he said to them, "Rob no one by violence or by false accusation, and be content with your wages."

¹⁵ As the people were in expectation, and all men questioned in their hearts concerning John, whether perhaps he were the Christ, ¹⁶ John answered them all, "I baptize you with water; but he who is mightier than I is coming, the thong of whose

sandals I am not worthy to untie; he will baptize you with the Holy Spirit and with fire. [17] His winnowing fork is in his hand, to clear his threshing floor, and to gather the wheat into his granary, but the chaff he will burn with unquenchable fire."

I want to call your minds today to some thoughts that cluster around the life and ministry of John Baptist. It has been my privilege through the summer to fulfill an assignment that involves some deep study in the Gospel of Luke and a study of the life of John Baptist. And the providences of my life just all worked together so that finally this man and his ministry have sort of become located for me.

You know, each of the four Gospels begins with the ministry of John Baptist, and I have wondered many times, "Where do we put him? Where does he belong? What slot does he go in? What place shall he fill? What is his thing?" I think about a pastor who was preaching a long, involved sermon on, "Where shall we put John the Baptist?" He was asking the question, "Does he belong in the Old Testament or the New?" Finally, one dear brother said, "He can have my place, I'm going home!"

Well, I finally found, I think, where to put him. And there is a word that goes with his ministry, and I'd like for you to look with me at Luke 1, beginning at verse 13. And I want to pick up some thoughts that gather around the message of this man.

Now Zechariah, the old priest, is doing his once-in-a-lifetime temple ministry, and the angel of the Lord comes to him and answers the deep prayer of his heart.

[13] . . . Do not be afraid, Zechari'ah, for your prayer is heard, and your wife Elizabeth will bear you a son, and you shall call his name John.

[14] And you will have joy and gladness,
and many will rejoice at his birth;
[15] for he will be great before the Lord,
and he shall drink no wine nor strong drink,
and he will be filled with the Holy Spirit,
even from his mother's womb.
[16] And he will turn many of the sons of Israel to the Lord their God,
[17] and he will go before him in the spirit and power of Eli'jah,
to turn the hearts of the fathers to the children,
and the disobedient to the wisdom of the just,
to make ready for the Lord a people prepared.
(Luke 1:13-17)

All of this ministry of John was to make ready a people **prepared**.

Now let's turn over to verses 67-68 of chapter 1. See, the angel said the first word to Zechariah before the birth of John Baptist. This is the word of Zechariah at the time of his birth. You remember, his tongue was loosed, and he blessed God, "[67] And his father Zechari'ah was filled with the Holy Spirit, and prophesied, saying, [68] 'Blessed be the Lord God of Israel, for he has visited and redeemed his people....'"

Then, down in verse 76, he speaks now to the child. "And you, child, will be called the prophet of the Most High; for you will go before the Lord to prepare his ways...."

There's that word again, "prepare." To make ready a people prepared. Now let's turn to Luke chapter 3, beginning in the last half of verse two.

> ² . . . The word of God came to John the son of Zechari'ah in the wilderness; ³ and he went into all the region about the Jordan, preaching a baptism of repentance for the forgiveness of sins. ⁴ As it is written in the book of the words of Isaiah the prophet,

> "The voice of one crying in the wilderness:
> Prepare the way of the Lord…." (Luke 3:2b-4a)

There's that word again. Before his birth, at his birth, and as he begins his ministry, the word is, "**Prepare** the way of the Lord!" Now what I'm about to say does not sound as profound as it has been to me, but here's what it is. **God prepares for the work that he does.**

Preparation is very significant in the economy of God! All four Gospels tell us before Jesus came, John Baptist was sent with the message of preparation to get ready for God's. Good. Thing. In fact, all of God's great things have been prepared for.

I think of Abraham, who was prepared to father the nation, and Moses was prepared to bring the people out of Egypt and make them the nation, the nation of God. Joshua prepared the people for the time of the Judges, the conquest of the land. Samuel prepared the people for the emergence of the monarchy and interpreted their times to them. Amos and Hosea interpreted the times and proclaimed the word of God and prepared the people for the exile or the demise of the Northern Kingdom, then Isaiah and Jeremiah and Ezekiel prepared the people, interpreted the times, and got them ready for the exile of the Southern Kingdom. And the minor prophets instructed them and interpreted the times and gave them the word of God as they rebuilt their nation. And then, as someone said, "The rivers of God flowed underground for those 400 years." And finally, God got ready to do the best thing he ever did in the sending of Jesus. And before God did the Best. Thing. He. Ever. Did, he sent John Baptist to get the people ready.

Now that's been kind of computing out in several directions in my life. I believe that this is not only an occasional situation, but I believe that there is an abiding, divine principle here. **God always gets ready for the good things he's going to do!**

Now I have to tell you where that meets me. There are times in my life, and I say that with the deep conviction that there are times in yours as well, when you have a growing hunger and a growing sense of need for God to do some good thing in your life. Do you understand that? There are times when we instinctively feel and know that God wants to do some good thing in our lives. Amen! Do you have those times now? A deep inner hunger for God to move into your life to do some good thing? Well, how do you get ready for it?

I have to tell you that the providence of God that triggered all this and brought it alive to me was the announcement that Dr. Brown made that Pasadena College is going to move to San Diego. You know, life had been moving along pretty good. You know, so-so, good times, bad times but alright. It's familiar, I like it, I'm happy as I can be. I happen to have a good home church [this one] and I'm happy in it and don't want to leave it, and all things are going along alright. I love what I'm doing, love the people I'm with...*most of the time.* And it's alright. And then here comes a memo: "Faculty meeting over in Science 102," so we all gather up and sit down and Dr. Brown opens up a thing and it says something like this, "The Board of Trustees of Pasadena College has entered into negotiations with Cal Western College for the purchase of their campus..." and I don't know what he said after that. You know, life is going along, everything is just like it was and then, "Boom"! You know, "The Board of Trustees has entered into negotiations...."

I think part of my problem is that nobody ever asked me! And I just can't understand how that can happen! But when it happened, I found myself entering into various negotiations, negotiations with myself, with my family, and with God. And God began to enter into negotiations with me! And I realized that this thing that had come into my life was God's good thing for me, for us, and God had given us a year to get ready for it.

And that same time I was studying about John Baptist, and I began to hear what he was saying and then asking myself, "How do God's good people get ready for God's good thing?" As I contemplate the future, I know some good thing needs to happen inside ME, and something good needs to happen to my FAMILY and in my family! And you can understand, can't you, that we all have a deep hunger for some good thing to happen to the College this year. I want God to do a good thing, and I think about us in our church and what it means to us, how all of us are involved in this. We want God to do a GOOD thing, don't we? And I hesitate to talk about the college situation, yet I don't mind because it is not only a fact, but it is a symbol of one of the GREAT facts of life, that into all of our lives things like this come. And God is working in all of them and wants to do Some. Good. Thing. Amen! How do we get ready for it?

Well, let's look at how John Baptist prepared the people for the best thing God ever did. Maybe it will help us find out how to get ready for the good thing he wants to do for us. Let's take a look, shall we?

In the passage that the pastor read earlier, I think all of us would agree that the message of John Baptist was basically a three-fold message. He preached judgment, and he preached repentance, and he preached ethics. Let's talk about that.

John Baptist preached **judgment**. Here came the Pharisees. All the crowds, the people, the groups within Judaism, there they came out to the wilderness to hear this radical preaching of John Baptist, and so he begins, as we see in verse 7b of Chapter 3. "You brood of vipers! Who warned you to flee from the wrath to come?"

I suppose that's very much like the pastor saying, "Good morning friends, we welcome you to our service this beautiful day."

No, he said, "You brood of vipers! Who warned you to flee from the wrath to come?"

The judgment of GOD is coming. He was saying to them, and to all of us, that the presence of JESUS always brings us under judgment! Now, I used to think that judgment was a bad, hard word. But anymore, I believe that it is a **good** and a **saving** word. Because apart from the judgment of God, There. Is. No. Salvation! Do we know that?

For example, here are the Pharisees, their neat patterns, their rationalized, accepted, compromised lifestyle. God had given the law, but they knew they couldn't keep it absolutely as it should be kept and so they had the

rationalizations and the
    compensations and the
        whole packaged deal and they had the
            rules that they went by
and they were pretty fairly happy with themselves. And there
they were, drifting along, and suddenly the word of God comes to
BREAK THROUGH, to EXPOSE the realities! But I tell you, only
in such exposing is there any salvation!

I don't know how to say that in the way that I feel it so that I can
communicate it with you. *I suppose I could yell it at you several times; I
don't know if that would help or not!*

Look, we also have our lifestyle. It isn't too good, but it isn't too bad,
you know. We're going along alright, could be better, but it could be
worse. We're getting along alright. And we've
    rationalized it and
        compromised it and
            we understand it and
                we can handle it, and
                    we can live with it
and so, life just moves on like it always has, sort of, and what needs
to happen is for GOD's verdict to break open the situation and reveal
it for what it is! Now, I'm not talking about judgment in the sense of
the final judgment, I'm talking about the verdict of God that needs
to fall upon our lives in
    revealing
        opening
            cleansing and
                healing ways.

Oh, I suddenly think of the rich man, who fared sumptuously every day, clothed in fine linen. He had his lifestyle, he had his life pattern, everything was worked out alright. In fact, the language of that passage would indicate that he was a Sadducee involved in the life of the Temple. Everything was alright, he was living magnificently. Outside his gate was a DYING BEGGAR! Somehow, he was able to walk to and fro, in and out of his house,

> compensate it
>> rationalize it
>>> adjust it and
>>>> compromise it

so that he could live with himself in his neat little lifestyle. And he lived magnificently right down to the time of his magnificent funeral, and he went to hell. Now that is NOT supposed to be the punch line, you know! God blesses his people, see, so here was the blessed person. What would have saved him? The judgment of God to break in upon that situation of his life, that accepted pattern of his life, and expose it to the healing light of God.

Then how do I get ready for God's good thing? The good thing I want him to do

> in my life,
>> my family,
>>> my school,
>>>> my home,
>>>>> my world,
>>>>>> my church?

I only know one way, and that is to open it up to God and let his verdict fall upon my life and my lifestyle. Can we let God help us do that? THAT'S how we get ready for God's good thing, praise the Lord!

Well, John preached another word. That word is **repentance**. And as judgment has a special meaning here in terms of God's verdict that falls upon us to reveal and open, so repentance has a special meaning here. He was speaking particularly to the Jewish people and he said to them, "Bring forth fruits meet for repentance and don't begin to say within yourselves, 'We have Abraham for our father.' The ax is laid to the root of the trees…" (Matt. 3:8-10a).

You want to talk about a radical message? He was talking to Jewish people. Look at their heritage, and John said, "DON'T say, we have Abraham"! I tell you, their heritage went back a long way, didn't it? Abraham and Isaac and Jacob and Joseph. And Moses and Joshua and Samuel and David and the prophets and, "what shall I more say for the time would fail me to tell of…" so and so and so and so… They had

> prophet and
> > priest and
> > > king and
> > > > Temple and
> > > > > ritual and
> > > > > > sacrifice.

All that whole line of precious heritage and history, which was the foundation of their self-image, and on their past, they based their hope and their security and John said, "The ax is laid to the root of the trees." Did you know that he cut them off From. Their. ROOTS?

Now what is this repentance that God demands of us, "Don't begin to say within yourselves, 'We have Abraham.'" Oh, he is calling for a radical release of the things we are depending upon. A turning away from All. False. Dependencies. That is radical, isn't it?

I don't know what we are saying to ourselves. What are our dependencies? I think if we'd all just take a moment of self-examination, we probably wouldn't come up with anything but God. I'm sure we'd all come up with the right answer until we just exposed our true selves.

I tell where this has been meeting me. I want to have a good year, and then I suddenly realize, I can't have a good year! How can we have a good year? What am I supposed to do as chaplain, run around and holify everything? I can't do that! What am I supposed to do, discern the times?

Make those keen decisions, plan

just the right things,

get just the right speakers,

do all the right stuff and

have a tremendous year?

Even when I say that, I KNOW it's an impossibility! What the Lord has been saying to me is, "Just come on back down boy." *I wish he wouldn't say that to me so often.* "Just come back down, it's all right. They're going to move this whole college and didn't even ask you. Just come on back down, boy, it's alright." That's a false dependency anyhow, isn't it?

Let's take a minute and look at Abraham. I think he's a marvelous symbol of this whole repentant spirit that helps us to cut ourselves off from false dependencies. Do you remember that God brought Abraham up from Ur of the Chaldees to Heron and separated him from his culture, his heritage, all of his past, his ancestry? There he separated him from his father's house and sent him down to the land of Palestine, cut free from ALL his past, and pointed toward God's future. And God gave Abraham Isaac as the sign of his promised future. "Abraham come out, come out and I will give you...." So, he cut him off from all his past, set him free to face the future

unencumbered,

unshackled,

unhindered,

no longer chained to his past;

and God gave him Isaac, the sign of that promised future, hallelujah!

And then one fine day God said, "Take your son, your only son, Isaac, whom you love, and offer him to me as a sacrifice on the mountain." Oh, God cut him off from his PAST and then God cut him off from his FUTURE, to let him know that his future did not rest with his own generation or his own ability to produce, or with anything God gave, but his future rested with GOD! Well Amen! Isn't that great?

Our future does not rest with our PAST! And our future does not rest with OUR future. God would cut us off from false dependencies to the past and false hopes and false dependencies for the future and let us know that our future is in the hands of GOD and not in the hands of anything he can give!

What is our future as a church? Where does it rest? In our ability to discern the times, to evaluate Pasadena? To make the projections to do all we ought to do so we won't miss the golden moment and fail in what God wants us to do? If that's the way it is, we've already had it! And that's true of my life, too.

The glory of this is that God would sever us from every false dependency and lock us into the kind of dependency upon himself, which really binds us to our true security and is our true hope. Praise the Lord!

I rejoice that our future does not rest on what we have been in Pasadena as a college, and thank God, it does not rest on San Diego. That's not where our hope is, is it? Where is our hope? Our hope is in God! Hallelujah! "Oh God, our help in ages past, our hope for years to come!" So, he would call us to a REPENTANT spirit that keeps turning away from the subtle and false dependencies of our lives.

And then one more thing John Baptist said, to them, and the Spirit says to us: God's people get ready for God's good thing by **lifting the ethical quality of their lives**. Praise the Lord!

The multitudes said, "What shall we do? God's getting ready to do his good thing. What shall we do?" And John said, "Be generous and give," Just. Like. That. The tax collectors came, "What shall we do?" "Be fair." "Is that all?" "Yes, that's all." And the soldiers came, and I wish they hadn't come, 'cause he said to them, "Don't bully, don't blackmail, don't throw your weight around and be content with your wages." God help us!

Now, when you begin to evaluate that, that's not any profound thing. That's just the same old stuff. C.S. Lewis talks about that "magnificent monotony of virtues" that have characterized the people of God throughout the centuries: selflessness, honesty, integrity. And so, the Spirit says to me, "Do you want God to do some good thing? Let the Spirit move out into your life to lift the ethical quality of it." Hallelujah!

Now, the worst part about this is that I can understand it, therefore, I have to deal with it. You remember when Naaman went to the prophet, and the prophet said, "Go down to the Jordan river and dip seven times"? And Naaman said, "I got better rivers at home!"

And so, he stomped off in a huff and his servant said to him, "If he'd asked you to do some hard thing, would you have done it? Then why don't you do this easy thing and be healed?" That's what God's been saying to me.

Here it is. I tell you this morning, I want God to do a good thing in my life, in the life of
> my family,
>> my home,
>>> my world,
>>>> my church.

How do I get ready? It's really
>>>> openness, and
>>> brokenness, and
>> repentance, and
> oneness

that expresses itself in the lifting of the ethical quality of my life.

Oh Lord Jesus, what do you want to say to us right now? What do you want to say to me? Teach me to know that it is not some far off esoteric thing that you desire. There is a good thing you are wanting to do, teach us how to prepare. Teach us to open up to the verdict of God. Teach the brokenness that separates us from all our false dependencies and return us to full dependence upon God. And then, Holy Spirit, reach out into the daily life that's ours, the multitudes, tax collectors, soldiers, wherever we are, and lift the ethical quality of our lives. In Jesus' name. Amen!

Sermon #4
Does God Still Create Anything New?
Various Scriptures

⟿

He preached this sermon across the country; the three tapes I have are from revivals held in Puyallup, Washington, Vicksburg, Michigan, and Naples, Florida. He began to focus on creation studies after he retired in 1989. I think his own life experiences, including his brain-damaged daughter Pamela and my divorce in 1986, were part of what fueled and informed his passion about new creation. God created something new when Scott Armstrong and I were married in July 1991.

I'd like to share some Scripture with you today; I'm going to start with Genesis 1, then I'm going to read from Psalm 40, Psalm 51, Isaiah 43, Isaiah 65, Jeremiah 31, Ezekiel 36, Romans 7, 2 Corinthians 5, and Revelation 21.

Now that you've found them all, let's proceed!

Actually, I'm going to read a bunch of verses from these chapters, and you can just follow along, but there's a question on my mind. Most of us here believe that God did something new in creation. The question I have is this, **Does God still create anything new?**

Genesis 1:1-3

> [1]In the beginning God created the heavens and the earth. [2]The earth was without form and void, and darkness was upon the face of the deep; and the Spirit of God was moving over the face of the waters.[3] And God said, "Let there be light"; and there was light.

In the beginning God created the heavens and the earth. What I want to know is, does he create anything new now? Any creation still going on?

Let's go to Psalm 40:1-3a

> [1]I waited patiently for the LORD;
> he inclined to me and heard my cry.
> [2]He drew me up from the desolate pit,
>   out of the miry bog,
> and set my feet upon a rock,
>   making my steps secure.
> [3]He put a new song in my mouth,
>   a song of praise to our God.

Now, let's go over to Psalm 51:10 where this theme is put into a prayer; these words that are familiar to many of us, I know.

> [10]Create in me a clean heart, O God,
>   and put a new and right spirit within me.

Now, let's go over to Isaiah 43:18-19a. *Aren't you glad we're doing this in order?*

> [18]Remember not the former things,
>   nor consider the things of old.

Did you hear that? No, you didn't. I'm tempted to say, "When are we going to start doing this?"

> [19] Behold, I am doing a new thing;
> now it springs forth, do you not perceive it?

Now let's go over to Isaiah 65:17

> [17] For behold, I create new heavens
> and a new earth;
> and the former things shall not be remembered
> or come into mind.

Now, let's go to Jeremiah 31:31-34

> [31] Behold, the days are coming, says the LORD, when I will make
> a new covenant with the house of Israel and the house of Judah,
> [32] not like the covenant which I made with their fathers when I
> took them by the hand to bring them out of the land of Egypt,
> my covenant which they broke, though I was their husband,
> says the LORD. [33] But this is the covenant which I will make with
> the house of Israel after those days, says the LORD: I will put
> my law within them, and I will write it upon their hearts; and I
> will be their God, and they shall be my people. [34] And no longer
> shall each man teach his neighbor and each his brother, saying,
> 'Know the LORD,' for they shall all know me, from the least
> of them to the greatest, says the LORD; for I will forgive their
> iniquity, and I will remember their sin no more.

Now, let's go to Ezekiel's version of that. It's found in vs. 36:26-27.
Ezekiel was down in Babylon and Jeremiah was up in Jerusalem, and
they are saying fundamentally the same thing. *I'm not insecure about reading
all of this because what I'm reading is better than anything I'm going to say!*

26 A new heart I will give you, and a new spirit I will put within you; and I will take out of your flesh the heart of stone and give you a heart of flesh. 27 And I will put my spirit within you, and cause you to walk in my statutes and be careful to observe my ordinances.

A new heart and a new spirit!

Now, let's go over to the New Testament, Romans 7:6.

6But now we are discharged from the law, dead to that which held us captive, so that we serve not under the old written code but in the new life of the Spirit.

Let' go on over to 2 Corinthians 5:17. Wonderful passage! *Well, all of them are, aren't they?*

17 Therefore, if anyone is in Christ, he is a new creation; the old has passed away, behold, the new has come. 18 All this is from God, who through Christ reconciled us to himself and gave us the ministry of reconciliation.

Well, if we're going to start with Genesis, let's wind up in Revelation 21:5.

5And he who sat upon the throne said, "Behold, I make all things new."

I have read you some words of God from the book of God and now, from the book of God, I'd like to read you some words from the book of man. Let's go to Ecclesiastes 1:9-10.

9What has been is what will be,
    and what has been done is what will be done;

and there is nothing new under the sun.
[10] Is there a thing of which it is said,
"See, this is new"?
It has been already,
in the ages before us.

Well, I think I think we've got a problem. You know, people like us, evangelical, religious, good people, *who are right, praise God*. People like us don't have a problem with the question, "Did God create the world?"

Now some among us are more literally inclined and like to think in terms of the action of God in six 24-hour days, and some think in more developmental, dynamic terms. But how ever we conceive it, folks like us don't have a problem with the question, "Did God create the heavens and the earth?"

My concern is, that's where our creation faith stops. We are locked-in to a mentality of cause-and-effect. Whether we like it or not, we're
children of the Enlightenment,
children of the Industrial Revolution,
children of the Scientific Revolution,
inheritors of and participants in the technological revolution,
we think "cause-and-effect."

It permeates how we perceive. We get it
at school,
at home,
in society,
in culture,
it comes to us through everything.

We absorb this mode: **this** produces **this, this** comes out of **that**, and the reason for **this** is **that**.

You know what I think? In terms of God starting everything, we believe in creation, but we have come to be evolutionists in how we think about what happened after that. How we think is "cause-and-effect."

I'd like for us to push this a little bit.

Let's say something terrible happens like,
a brain-damaged child is born,
or a divorce tears up a family,
or some sinful act or some terrible habit pattern destroys a
    home or a
    marriage or a
    dream,
or booze and drugs bring somebody down to the pits,
or economic reversal or bankruptcy tear up a life.

But then, after a time, out of these tragedies, there comes a new sense of compassion, a new sense of mission to the hurting and the damaged.

Out of a terrible divorce there emerges a new and beautiful relationship.

Or out of a terrible, destructive life pattern brought to the bottom by drink or drugs comes a ministry, an influence, maybe a speaking platform and books that bless many.

So, we look back and we say, "Well, maybe that wasn't as bad as we thought it was. See, how out of this terrible divorce, a new and wonderful thing has emerged?" Or "Out of a life that has been destroyed, a ministry has come!"

And so, we say, "Maybe God let this happen so that out of it he could bring this. Maybe it looks bad, but it really isn't." Or "Maybe God just let somebody go to the bottom because look how new life has come!" *Now don't anybody say, "Amen"!*

And we say, "Maybe divorce isn't really all that bad, look what came out of it! Maybe what looked like a tragedy was some way of bringing about this wonderful new thing!"

NO! NO!

Folks, if something good comes out of something bad, it doesn't come out of what's bad! It is because GOD HAS DONE A NEW AND CREATIVE THING! Hallelujah!

Remember **not** the former things!
> A **new** heart
>> A **new** song
>>> A **new** spirit
>>>> A **new** creation
>>>>> Praise God!

My old granddad would say, "Are you a'catchin' on?"

I'm talking to a bunch of people who believe in creation but who are evolutionists in their thinking. And I'm not saying that's a bad word, it's a neutral word. But we think cause-and-effect.

Let's turn that over. I have a suspicion I'm talking to somebody who's looking back on something tragic—
the loss of a husband or a wife,
or, *dear Lord*, the loss of a child,
or a mother or a father,
or a dream, or a job, or health,
or abuse, or hard times…

And we look back and say, "If only that hadn't happened!" "If only I'd made another choice!" "**This** has happened in my life, and now I'm locked-in to **this**."

Do you know people who feel like, "You know, when I was young, the Lord called me to the mission field, and I didn't go, and I wasn't walking close to the Lord and then I've had to be content with second best all the rest of my life."? *Anybody not know what I'm talking about?*

"If I'd made a better decision, if I'd done differently, if this hadn't happened,
then my life would have had meaning,
my life would have had value,
I could have fulfilled my dreams but, you see,
because **this** happened that means **this**, and
because that happened, I won't be able…and
I wish I could, but it just never did work out and so,
I don't have the meaning and the future that I could have."

NO! NO!

God says, "Remember NOT the former things!" God is creative! GOD CREATES A NEW THING! *Can we see that?*

I think most of us are locked-in to Ecclesiastes: "There is nothing new under the sun!" And we are caught in this horizontal, rational, logical, cause-and-effect syndrome.

And the word of God comes into this and says, "Behold,
> I do a **new** thing
>> A **new** song
>>> A **new** heart
>>>> A **new** spirit
>>>>> A **new** creation!"

I've come to believe that God wants to create in us a creation mentality to replace our cause-and-effect mentality. Folks, creation means creation, and only GOD can create.

And I'm talking to people who believe with all their hearts that God created at the beginning of the world but view themselves as
> locked-in to the past,
>> locked-in to the way it is,
>>> locked-in to their genes,
>>>> locked-in to their hormones.

Friends, God is creative and creates a NEW thing! Do you believe that?

I'm not trying to be simplistic, and nobody's dumb enough to think that what happened to us before has no effect upon us, but I think we're dumber if we think that what happened before determines everything that we are going to be because God is still CREATING! God still creates something **NEW!**

A **new** heart

A **new** spirit

A **new** song

A **new** life

A **new** place to stand

and, *thank God*, a **new** heaven and earth to go around it!

Oh, praise the Lord!

Do you remember when Nicodemus came to Jesus by night, and Jesus said to him, "Nicodemus, you must be born again"? I'm fascinated by his response, "Can a man go back when he is old to his mother's womb and be born again?"

You see where Nicodemus was coming from? Even back in the 1st century! He was hearing something new, but you see where he was locked-in? "Can a man go back?" He knew better, but he was locked-in to cause-and-effect: the reason **this** is, is because of **that** and the reason **that** is, is because of **this**.

And when Jesus said, "You can be born anew," Nicodemus brought it right down to the process of cause-and-effect and Jesus had to get him unhinged from that. And you know what I'm praying today is that the Holy Spirit will help us to get unhinged from the way WE think about cause-and-effect.

There are a couple of things I like about this. One is that the word "creation" is a good word. When you talk creation, you're talking something only God can do, right? That's God's thing, it's out of our control, we can't preempt it, it's God's prerogative.

The other word I like is "new." *Oh, praise the Lord!* "New" is a good word. And when "new" is the word going with creation, it means that God does more than reconfigure the puzzle pieces of our lives. God does more than simply re-structure the tinker toys of our lives. *Or, if you're not as old as I am, I suppose it would be the Lego pieces.* Do you know God does more than re-shuffle the Rook cards life has dealt us? *Those are the only kind of cards folks like us really know about!*

I think this is a significant thing. What does God do? Re-shuffle the deck? Re-shuffle the dominoes? Re-structure the old Tinker Toys?

The word of God is, "Behold, I'm doing a **new** thing! See, it springs forth!" Amen!

If we can really believe that God still creates something new, we are released from bondage to our past by our perceptions of it.

You know what I think binds us to our past? How we perceive it. I'm not sure it's so much what happened in our past as how we perceive what happened in our past, how we evaluate it. And so, we say, "Oh, something terrible happened, and life could be **thus**, and **thus**, and **thus**, except for **that**."

But if we believe God does a new thing, we are not bound to our perceptions of the past whether they are good or bad, whether they are accurate or inaccurate.

We are released, and we don't have to say, "Oh, that was so awful!" Or we don't have to say, "Maybe it wasn't as awful I thought it was," or "Maybe somehow it just finds its place in the great plan of God..." *Oh, give me a break!*

Somebody said, "This is just God's next stage in the unfolding of his perfect plan…" *I'm kind of nervous now… I wish I knew you better!*

And I'm telling you, our perceptive world is our REAL world and it has POWER! And we look back and we say, "Oh well, divorce may not be all that bad because something good came out of it." *Bah humbug!*

What's good that comes out of it, if anything does, is a **gift of grace**!

Or we look back and we say, "It was terrible, lousy, rotten, no good, awful…," *and if you've been through something like that, you've got a lot better words than these to describe it, some of which you don't usually say in church!* So, all the rest of your life is all messed up because…

So, we evaluate it and we interpret it and we apply it and it controls our present. But the truth is, **this** DOESN'T create **this**… Whatever is new is a **gift** of God. It is a **creation** of God, and I am free from the bondage of rationalizing, explaining, defending, defining. Amen!

You'll have to forgive me for being so old. It isn't my fault. I was born at a very young age a long time ago. I've been around long enough to know that when I look out over a group of people who are all dressed up to come to church, and look so nice and holy, I am not the only one who carries pain that doesn't go away. I'm not the only one who cares about my family.

I said to Mary Jo, "If our kids are so great, how come we're layin' in the bed cryin'?" Well, they are great, and we're still layin' in the bed cryin'! And I'm old enough not to be sensitive about that because I'm looking at people who have a story like mine.

Maybe your divorce wasn't so bad, maybe it was far worse than you could ever have dreamed! And talking to some of you who are bound up in the present because of how you are interpreting your past.

And the wonder of God's creation is "Behold, I do a NEW thing." Hallelujah! "Remember NOT the former things." Praise the Lord!

The truth is, if God creates a new thing, we can let the past be what it is.

If it's awful, it's awful;
> if it's great, it's great;
>> what's terrible is terrible;
>>> what's tragic is tragic;
>>>> what's sinful is sinful;
>>>>> what's beautiful is beautiful.

And it's in the hands of God and we are RELEASED from the past *and you know where I'm going now*, and we are OPEN to the future. Praise the Lord! If God creates a new thing, you see what direction that points us? Toward the FUTURE!

Now the verses I read to you this morning, *this may come as a surprise to you*, they can be found in any good concordance under the heading, "New." *I mean, preachers shouldn't really tell those hidden secrets.* Let's take just a minute and look at the context of some of them.

You know, the context of Genesis 1 is the primordial chaos, the darkness over the face of the deep. And the Spirit of God is moving over the abyss and out of the darkness God brought order and beauty and life and meaning until he could look and say, "It's good!"

And I'm talking to some of you who know about the waters of darkness and chaos. And I'm telling you, God is CREATIVE, and the Holy Spirit of God can brood over the face of the waters of our lives and bring beauty for ashes and the oil of joy for mourning.

I tell you, whatever else creation means, it means there's a future, right? Creation means POSSIBILITY! Praise the Lord!

Psalm 40,

> ² *He drew me up from the desolate pit,*
> *out of the miry bog,*
> ³ *He put a new song in my mouth,*
> *a song of praise to our God.*

Look at Psalm 51, do you see the context there? We're talking lust and adultery and murder and at a point of total inability and total failure, God answers the cry, "Create in me a clean heart and renew a right spirit within me." And there's openness to a FUTURE! Not because of how we reevaluate the past, but because we are RELEASED from the past to move on into the new creation.

Do you remember Jeremiah 31, when God said to Jeremiah, "I'll make a new covenant"? Israel had strained and pushed and pulled the covenant until it was broken and gone. And when hope was gone and nothing was left, do you know what God said? "I got a thought. I'm going to do something brand-new! Do you know what I'm going to do? They can't even live the way they ought to live. You know what I'm going to do? I'm going to forgive them!" You want to talk new, folks? We're talkin' NEW! "I'm going to put a new spirit in them." We're talking CREATION, folks, *aren't we?* And we're RELEASED from the past!

And you remember in Ezekiel, when the people of God were down
in Babylon

    in the ghetto,

        in the big pagan city,

            with the big, big walls.

                No hope,

            no help,

        no life,

    right there,

God said, "I will do a NEW thing!"

And right at the point of Paul's struggling with the law, with legalism,
trying to do right, trying to be right, was the marvelous liberty in
Christ, "So that we serve not under the old written code but in the
NEW life of the Spirit." Praise God!

"Therefore, if anyone be in Christ, he is a **NEW** creation." *Folks,
that's in the book! Actually, it's been there several years now.*

And then in Revelation, "he who sat on the throne..." Well, who's
sitting on the throne? If you want to follow through the imagery of
Revelation, it's the Lord who is the Lamb slain from the foundation
of the world, who through his marvelous redemption has triumphed
over the ancient inveterate forces of evil seen in their great worldwide
depth and malignancy.

Oh! Do you know what he says? "Behold I make all things NEW!
Praise God!

Do you know why we can talk like this? The reason we can have the
temerity to affirm such marvelous reality in the face of this old tired
and bored world is that God did a BRAND-NEW THING when he

created the heavens and the earth! Did you know that that had never been done before? That was the first time that had ever happened! What do you think of that?

Do you know why we can talk like this? Because God did a marvelous NEW THING when he broke the power of the Egyptian empire and set his rag tags and nobodies free! That had never, ever been done before on land or sea!

Do you know why we can talk like this? Because God did a marvelous NEW THING in the incarnation! There is nothing like that in all the world.

Do you know why we can affirm such things? Because God did an awful, awesome, NEW THING when he himself in Jesus came to die for us on the cross!

And we can talk this way because God did a shattering, wondrous, NEW THING in raising Jesus from the dead and exalting him to the right hand of glory!

And so, out of our darkness out of our failures and our past, there comes a wondrous, wondrous word, **God. Still. Creates. Something. NEW!** Amen!

This allows us to receive the creative gift of God into our present, which sets us free to go on not by rationalizing, defining, explaining, or proverb-ing, *Oh God, save us from proverbs! (I don't mean the book.)*

You know, when something happens and you say, "Well, every cloud has a silver lining!" *I want to say, "Shut up!"*

"Well, God has a reason." *"Oh, come on!"*

"Well God did **this**…so **that**." *"Oh, did he now?"* *When did we get the gift of second-guessing God?*

God wants to set us free from being boxed-in to this dead-end street that I believe

> stifles our vitality
>> muffles our clear voice
>>> frustrates our creativity
>>>> and so, we have neither great joy nor freedom.

What's helping me is to begin to believe that **God. Is. Creative**! In my life, in your life, God sets before us his creative power and we don't have to live our lives by

> redefining the past or
>> analyzing or
>>> excusing or
>>>> defending or
>>>>> ignoring.

It's in the hands of God, and God can do a NEW THING, Praise the Lord!

Well, I almost said a dumb thing. I almost said, do you need something new? That's a dumb question, isn't it? Let me rephrase it, what new thing do you need God to do for you? What old thing do you need to be released from?

I pray that the Holy Spirit will help us to get unhinged from our old cause-and-effect system. Friends, the law of cause-and-effect in Christ is hereby ANNULLED!

And God is free of our manipulation, and our lives are liberated from our need to define them or defend them because **God. Still. Creates. Something. NEW!** Amen!

"Something Beautiful"
Words and music: Bill and Gloria Gaither

Prayer: Oh Father, we thank you, we are so grateful that having created the world you're not locked-in to it. And having failed you, we're not locked-in either. We praise you. Will you help us not to define and analyze and interpret our past so much? But to realize that we can surrender to you all of it and walk on into a future that is your new creation with thanks and joy. Amen!

Sermon #5
When God Contradicts God
Genesis 22:1–14

This sermon was preached at one of the San Diego Nazarene churches in the early '90s (it was likely preached earlier; it's so well crafted). Whichever church it was, they were between pastors, and Dad alludes to that situation. He sent me a copy of the recording in 2003, when we were living in northeast Ohio after resigning our faculty positions at Northwest Nazarene University for Scott to take a position at Baldwin Wallace College. We moved back to Ohio primarily to be closer to his mom and our son and daughter-in-law, who were living in the Columbus area. I sensed a call to full-time pastoral ministry and left academia fully expecting to find a position there in the Cleveland area but, to that point, and to my dismay, had found nothing.

Would you open up your Bibles with me to the 22nd chapter of Genesis?

> [1] After these things God tested Abraham, and said to him, "Abraham!" And he said, "Here am I." [2] He said, "Take your son, your only son Isaac, whom you love, and go to the land of Mori'ah, and offer him there as a burnt offering upon one of the mountains of which I shall tell you." [3] So Abraham rose early

in the morning, saddled his ass, and took two of his young men with him, and his son Isaac; and he cut the wood for the burnt offering, and arose and went to the place of which God had told him. [4] On the third day Abraham lifted up his eyes and saw the place afar off. [5] Then Abraham said to his young men, "Stay here with the ass; I and the lad will go yonder and worship and come again to you." [6] And Abraham took the wood of the burnt offering, and laid it on Isaac his son; and he took in his hand the fire and the knife. So, they went both of them together. [7] And Isaac said to his father Abraham, "My father!" And he said, "Here am I, my son." He said, "Behold, the fire and the wood; but where is the lamb for a burnt offering?" [8] Abraham said, "God will provide himself the lamb for a burnt offering, my son." So, they went both of them together.

[9] When they came to the place of which God had told him, Abraham built an altar there, and laid the wood in order, and bound Isaac his son, and laid him on the altar, upon the wood. [10] Then Abraham put forth his hand and took the knife to slay his son. [11] But the angel of the LORD called to him from heaven, and said, "Abraham, Abraham!" And he said, "Here am I." [12] He said, "Do not lay your hand on the lad or do anything to him; for now I know that you fear God, seeing you have not withheld your son, your only son, from me." [13] And Abraham lifted up his eyes and looked, and behold, behind him was a ram, caught in a thicket by his horns; and Abraham went and took the ram, and offered it up as a burnt offering instead of his son. [14] So Abraham called the name of that place The LORD will provide; as it is said to this day, "On the mount of the LORD it shall be provided."

Oh my, isn't that a story? One of the most profound experiences in all the whole Bible. Really, you know, there are four persons involved, and not just three. God is involved, oh yes! Abraham is involved and Isaac is involved, and **we ourselves** are involved. Those who read and those who hear are involved in this story.

And you know, we see it from two perspectives. On the one hand, we are brought into the gallery, and we observe the terrible drama that's going on. But at the same time, we are drawn down into the arena and we accompany Abraham and Isaac on their agonizing journey.

And, you know, we understand a little bit in advance how the story is going to come out. We know that God is testing Abraham and that he, indeed, passes the test, but really it doesn't do much to relieve our anxiety. The suspense is not lessened because we know a little bit. See, we have some clue about what's happening, but Abraham doesn't. And we want to cry out, "Abraham!" and hear him say for the fourth time, "Here am I." We want to say, "Abraham, it's going to be alright!" But we cannot, and we can only suffer with him in helplessness and silence while he suffers his terrible ordeal. What a story!

Let's go back and take a look at it. I'd like for us to look at the story a little bit and then let's let the story look at us for a little bit.

You know, Abraham has just received a confirming word in chapter 21, "for through Isaac shall your descendants be named". And then in chapter 22, one awful, awful day, God breaks into their idyllic life. After all the struggles that Abraham has gone through, they are in the period of tranquility and that is shattered by the awful voice of God, "Abraham!" And Abraham says, "Here am I." One commentator says that a good paraphrase of that would be, "Ready!"

And God says to Abraham (*listen to this, it's called "turning the knife"*), "Take your son, your only son, Isaac, **whom you love**, and offer him to me on a mount I will show you."

Early in the morning... *It's a good thing he didn't talk it over with Sarah, isn't it? He'd have never got out of the house!* Early in the morning he saddles the pack animals, *God knows what he says to his young men, or to Isaac,* loads up the animals, and cuts the wood.

Have you ever cut wood? Can you see that? Can you hear that? And you wonder, "What is this man thinking?" He takes the wood, gets the fire and a knife, a better translation is a cleaver, *as in a meat cleaver,* and they begin the journey.

Three days! It's awesome what we're not told! Three. Silent. Days. of journey. What is going on?

And then Abraham sees the mountain. And he says to his young men, "Stay here, the lad and I will go." And the two of them walk on together.

Well, how old was Isaac? Old enough to carry wood, old enough to go on the journey, old enough to ask the question, "My father," "Here am I, my son." "We have the wood and the fire, but where's the lamb?" And Abraham's enigmatic answer reflects both his own faith and his own wonderment. And I think we sense that Isaac is beginning to get the feeling that maybe he knows...and they walk on, the two of them together.

And then the narrative just slows down. It's like a series of slides. Can you see it? Abraham built an altar there, and laid the wood in order, and bound Isaac, and laid him on the altar, upon the wood.

Then it slows down to individual scenes... Abraham puts forth his hand and takes the knife... "But the angel of the LORD called to him from heaven, and said, 'Abraham, Abraham!' And he said, 'Here am I.' He said, 'Do not lay your hand on the lad or do anything to him; for now I know that you fear God, seeing you have not withheld your son, your only son, from me.'"

And the ordeal is over. And there is the ram caught in the thicket.

Well, the question I have is, what in the world is going on here? What's happening in this story? I'll tell you what's happening here,
>   God is contradicting GOD!
>   Faith is contradicting FAITH!
>   And command is contradicting PROMISE!

Well, here's the promise... "I will make of you a great nation. Through Isaac shall your descendants be named!" There's the promise. Oh, that's a promise worth leaving HOME for! That's a promise worth LIVING for! And when you put it together with all that goes around those few words of promise, that's enough to HOPE for! That's enough to LIVE for! Thank God for the promise!

And then one awful day comes the terrible word of God, "Take your son, your only son Isaac, whom you love and offer him to ME." God is contradicting God!

Well, let's look at it this way. God had cut Abraham off from his past. Remember in Genesis 12, God said to him, "Go from your country and your kindred and your father's house." See what all he had to leave?

"Leave it all behind!" He cut him off from
    his country,
        his culture,
            his extended family,
                his genealogy.
He cut him off from his father's house and gave him a hope and a
future!

God, at the awful time of mankind's history of alienation and
estrangement and loss, called Abraham and made a promise, and in that
promise God intended to begin a saving history that would lead ultimately
    to Calvary,
        to the resurrection,
            to the outpouring of the Holy Spirit,
                and to the **saving of the world!**

And God cuts Abraham off from his past, and points him to that
glorious future, and then finally, finally, finally, after years of futile,
fervent hope, and long agonizing delay, the promise is fulfilled, and
Isaac is born. Here is Isaac, the embodiment of the promise! Can
you see that?

God cuts Abraham off from his past and points him toward the
future, and then finally, finally, Isaac is born who embodies in
himself the hopes... *I started to say, "the hopes and fears of all the years,"*
and for Abraham, they were in Isaac.

And then on that awful day, God cuts Abraham off. From. His.
Future! And says, "Give me your son." I think those lines are just
terrible! "Take your son, your only son, Isaac, Whom. You. Love."
And God cuts him off from his future.

Now I think we already know, but let's rehearse this for just a moment. Isaac is more than the idolized son of an old and doting father. He was that alright, *remember that phrase, "whom you love,"* but Isaac is more than that. Isaac is the embodiment of the promise! Isaac is the one through whom the line will go on.

When God began to save the world through Abraham, he called a man without a future…Sarah was barren, she had no child. And in the face of that awful futility and hopelessness, God makes a promise, and thank God, it comes true. And when all is well, God says, "Take him!" You see, Isaac is not only a beloved son, he is the symbol of God's **promise**!

Have you ever wondered why God didn't say, "Take Ishmael"? or "Take all your cattle"? Or "Take all your riches"? No, it was Isaac, the child of the promise.

And I wish I knew what was going on here. *And remember, I don't understand this stuff, I just teach it!* If you think you've got troubles with this passage, so do I! What is going on here? Well for one thing, when God contradicts God, he is teaching Abraham. *I wonder if **we** can learn*, that the future does not rest with anything God gives, but the future rests with God.

That's almost like dying! You see, God cut him off from his PAST and then God cut him off from his FUTURE to let him know that his future was not with Isaac, the future is not with the gifts, but the future is with **GOD**. And in this story, we ourselves hear, as I think Abraham did, a radical call to make the distinction between the gifts and the giver.

I think we understand, don't we, that the gifts we have received, *and I don't want to interpret that, I don't know what I mean by all of that,* but what God has given, the gifts God has given to us have a way of taking on a life of their own. And we have a way of depending upon the things God has given to us.

And so, the word comes to Abraham, "Take your son."
What if Isaac is lost? What then?
What if the people of God end up in exile down in Babylon and lose their land? What then?
What if the Savior of the world ends up on a cross between two thieves? What then?
Is all lost?

Oh, thank God, NO, it is not lost! But what happens is, we are called back, as Abraham was, as Israel was.

Have you ever wondered why they told this terrible story? Why did they keep telling that story around the campfire? Terrible story! Oh my! God is contradicting God, and in the mystery of that contradiction between what God seems to have given and what he seems to withdraw, somewhere in there we are taught that our future does not rest with Anything. God. Gives!

And the Holy Spirit would call us back to recognize that folks like you and me, who by the grace of God are called to live in the covenant; folks like us need to know that our hope, our future doesn't rest with anything God gives, but with God himself!

Now you know that I do not have any personal rights to say what I'm about to say, *which seldom keeps a preacher from saying what he's gonna say!* But I really have been hearing this and I believe it is a word from

God. And I need to say to you out of this story that the future of this body of believers does not rest with anything God gives. *Now if I were in my own church fellowship I would say, "C'mon now, nod your little heads and say, 'Amen.'"*

Did you know the future of this fellowship does not rest on your ability to discern the times or interpret the demographics, or to project the ways it ought to go? *I'm so old I'm going to say, "Give it up!"*

Do you want to know some wonderful, wonderful news? The future of this body of believers does not rest upon any of God's gifts. And in this community of believers there are many, aren't there? But folks, the future does not rest on what God gives us, the future rests on God himself. And like Abraham, WE are called, in the mystery and in the contradictions of our lives, to offer back to God what he has given, for him to use in his ways.

And, of course, I can't help thinking about our own lives, about mine and about yours. There are times when God contradicts God, aren't there? I'm talking to some of you who have felt like you received a promise, a door's been opened, you know, something has been given and all is well. And then for reasons we cannot discern, there is loss or the door closes.

For instance, we have dear friends who were ready to go the mission field, and in the health exam before going discovered that she had leukemia. And life has been a struggle all the way. They never made it to the field.

Anyone identify with that? I understand that. I don't like it, but I sure understand it.

And here is a PROMISE,
>   here is a HOPE,
>   here is a FUTURE!

And don't you wish that what God took away you had the assurance
that he would give back?!

When I was chaplain at the college, I do believe I talked to a
hundred young people in this situation. I talked to this girl who
really needed just to give up this guy and the only hitch was that
she knew, and so did I, that if she really gave him up there was no
guarantee that she'd get him back again.

That's what makes this story so poignant because Abraham didn't
know either, did he? All he knew was that God had made him a
promise and now he was contradicting it and there are ways in which
each of us, in the mystery of
>   our own lives,
>   our own hearts,
>   our journeys,
>   our hurts,
>   our hopes and dreams,

know what it means to feel like you have divine guidance, divine
promise, and then to have it
>   frustrated,
>   stifled,
>   closed off…

Well, what do you do when God contradicts God? Well, I get help
from Abraham. You know what he did? He obeyed the command
and believed the promise! Amen!

When the mystery is terrible, when it's awful, in the face of the contradictions and inequities, what do you do? I'll tell you what, keep on believing! Amen! Keep on obeying!

And, you know, we can say that **not** because we have the strength of Abraham to pass all our tests, but we can say that because on another mountain, another son trusted his father's promise and obeyed his father's will, and this son was **not** spared at the last moment. "He that spared not his own son but delivered him up for us all, how shall he not with him also freely give us all things?" (Rom. 8:32).

And the wonderful thing is that when God contradicts God, there is a place to go.

It's back to the **cross**!

Back to the place of surrender.

Back to the place of obedience.

Back to the place of trust

where in identification with Jesus there, oh praise God, we find life and strength to live in obedience and live in faith in the midst of the contradictions, in the sure knowledge that God. Will. Provide. Amen!

Don't you like the way the writer of Hebrews interprets it? "He that had received the promise offered up his only begotten son, of whom it was said that in Isaac shall thy seed be called, accounting that God was able to raise him up, even from the dead!" (Heb. 11:17b-19a).

Oh! Then out of hopelessness there's hope, because God. Will. Provide. Amen! Praise God!

Do you believe that? *No, you're just being nice, you're always nice in church.*
It isn't easy, is it?

Am I talking to anybody this morning who needs to give back the
gifts you've been depending on and put your faith in God? I wonder
if I'm talking to anyone for who the gifts of God have become more
precious than God?

And even though it breaks his heart, God would lead us to the
mountain to let us know our hope is in him, and not in anything else.

I pray this morning that you'll be helped by the Holy Spirit, that we
all will, to offer to God
> our trust,
>> our faith,
>>> our obedience,
>>>> the gifts that he's given us,
>>>>> the idols of our hearts
to trust him and obey him in the mystery of our lives. Because he
knows what he's doing, and he'll see us through. Amen!

Would you stand with me? As we close, I want us to read together
these words from hymn #107.

"Be not dismayed whate'er betide; God will take care of you.
Beneath his wings of love abide; God will take care of you.

Through days of toil when your heart doth fail; God will take care of
you.
When dangers fierce your path assail; God will take care of you."

4ᵗʰ verse

"No matter what may be the test, God will take care of you.
Lean, weary one, upon his breast; God will take care of you."

Oh my! Do you believe that? Praise God! That's true, isn't it? Let's sing the chorus.

Chorus

"God will take care of you, thro' every day, o'er all the way.
He will take care of you; God will take care of you."

"God Will Take Care of You"
Words: Civilla D. Martin, 1904
Music: W. Stillman Martin, 1904

Folks, if that's true, that's about the best news we ever heard in the midst of the mysteries and contradictions of our human existence! Amen!

Sermon #6
Ordinary Life
Philippians 2:19–30

This sermon was preached at Pasadena First Nazarene Church. The tape wasn't dated, but it is clear from the contents that it was after the departure of Rev. Earl G. Lee, longtime pastor and dear friend of my dad's. Dad preached numerous Sundays in the interim before their new pastor, Rev. H. B. London, came in 1985.

Let's begin in Philippians at Chapter 2, verse 19.

> [19] I hope in the Lord Jesus to send Timothy to you soon, so that I may be cheered by news of you. [20] I have no one like him, who will be genuinely anxious for your welfare. [21] They all look after their own interests, not those of Jesus Christ. [22] But Timothy's worth you know, how as a son with a father he has served with me in the gospel. [23] I hope therefore to send him just as soon as I see how it will go with me; [24] and I trust in the Lord that shortly I myself shall come also.

²⁵ I have thought it necessary to send to you Epaphroditus my brother and fellow worker and fellow soldier, and your messenger and minister to my need, ²⁶ for he has been longing for you all, and has been distressed because you heard that he was ill. ²⁷ Indeed he was ill, near to death. But God had mercy on him, and not only on him but on me also, lest I should have sorrow upon sorrow. ²⁸ I am the more eager to send him, therefore, that you may rejoice at seeing him again, and that I may be less anxious. ²⁹ So receive him in the Lord with all joy; and honor such men, ³⁰ for he nearly died for the work of Christ, risking his life to complete your service to me.

Well, if you were looking for a golden text in that passage, I hope you found one. As a matter of fact, I haven't. Which is actually why I want to talk about it today. Let me begin with a question. I've had the privilege of being with you here for several Sundays and, as I recall, we haven't had any guilt at all, hardly. So, today's the day for a little guilt, alright?

Here's the question. If your life were really all that it ought to be in the Lord, if you were really walking with the Lord the way you ought to be, if you were filled with the Spirit the way you ought to be, *c'mon now folks, we got a little guilt here.* If you were really what you ought to be with God, if you really had the Holy Spirit, if you really were the kind of Christian you know God wants you to be, what do you think your life would be like? I think that's a very good question to think about once in a while. What do you think your life would be like?

Well, I think there are some who feel like if you really are what God wants you to be, you'll carry around a nine-pound Bible with an *ichthus* on it. Or, you'll always be running off to religious conferences and seminars, or you'll be into journaling and you'll carry around your notebook, or you'll be memorizing Scripture all the time. Or, if you're older, you'll listen to holy records all day. *We shall not speak of religious radio broadcasts or T.V. ministries.* Your prayers would be answered, doors would be opened, you'd be vibrant and vital, etc., etc., etc.

Did you ever meet somebody and you said, "How are you doing?" and they said, "Oh, I'm just praising the Lord!" I always just want to say, "Will you just shut up! Why don't you just tell me how you are?" There are some who feel like they need to talk holy language, that spiritual life and holy language go together. *You already know what side I'm on, so we'll just go ahead.*

I remember walking with a guy from the religion building down to chapel some years ago. He was a really great guy, probably a sophomore. *I just love sophomores—they've been to college for nine months, they've read half a book, and they know all things. They are a wondrous breed, I love 'em.* We were walking down to chapel and he said to me, "Oh Brother Welch, I was just travailing in prayer before the Lord, last night." I mean, this kid was probably about 19 and I thought, "I bet you can't even spell it!" But, he had had a genuine experience of fellowship and prayer and that needed to be shared, but it had to be shared in holy language.

Is that the way it is? When it comes right down to it, what do you think the Christian life would be like if, in fact, you really were what God wanted you to be? Well, I'd like to share with you two things that come out of this passage to me. One is the conviction that the Christian life, after all, is quite ordinary and that if you were all that God wanted you to be, it just could be that your life would be pretty much the way it is now. Is that alright? When you just think about it, the way Christians live their lives and the way other human beings live their lives is pretty much the same, wouldn't you say? Most folks have to get up in the morning, have to go to the bathroom, have to eat, have to go to work, have to take care of stuff, which I think is pretty much the way humans are.

I'm concerned about this because I've come to think that sometimes, in our desire to be spiritual, or our desire to be what God wants us to be, we can, in fact, put God against God. And in our hunger to be spiritual, we can deny two of the great fundamentals of our faith. *I'm just sharing with you what's alive in my own thought processes these days.* But you know there is a doctrine, it's the most wonderful doctrine in the world, it's called the doctrine of **creation**!

We really believe in creation, don't we? Now, don't misunderstand me, I'm not interested in creation-ism, I have no concern about whether it was six days or where the bones of Adam are, 'cause I don't think Genesis cares about that. But I'll tell you what I believe the Bible really cares about; it is that we are the **creatures** of God, that our world is the **creation** of God, we are the **people** of God, made in his image. And in spite of all that's wrong with it, it's a good old world our good old God made! Isn't it? And it's good to be, it's good to live, good to smell the flowers, and enjoy the view, and know that God is God, and let our weight down on the world the way it is!

I just love the Genesis story. God said, "Let there be!" and it was so, and God said, "That's GOOD!" There was evening and there was morning. And the next day God said, "Let there be!" and it was so, and God said, "That's GOOD!" Then God created all the animals and Adam looked them all over and named them all and said, "Hmm." And then God made Eve, and Adam said, "Now we are gettin' somewhere!" And when he got all done, God said, "That's VERY GOOD!" And then God blessed them; God looked down on the whole thing and just blessed them. Amen! And, you know, if in order to be holy you have to get away from the world the way it is, DON'T PUT GOD AGAINST GOD, because God made it!

The other great fundamental doctrine for us is **incarnation**, which means that the eternal, sovereign God himself entered into life the way he'd made it. It's just awesome to me to realize that when God wanted to do the best thing he ever did, he just came into our world in a body. When God came to save our souls, he took on a body. When he came to forgive our sins, and to give us new life, he came down into a world that's Just. Like. Ours. And it wasn't like a fairy tale, no flowers opening or birds singing, no, he just came right down into our world the way it was.

He grew up all those years working in a carpenter's shop; you **know** he hit his thumb with a mallet! And he must have said, "shalom." *Well, he wouldn't say sheol, now would he?* It's awfully hard for us to just let God down into the world, isn't it?

Think about this, what's the most precious gift God can give us? Well, probably children. Now, what's the hardest thing on our religion, in the whole world? Children! Now that's weird, isn't it? Listen, I had experience and doctrine, clear, all put together, and then we had children—it just blew everything apart!

I've come to the great conclusion that if you have little children, do not, I repeat, do not try to be holy. Give it up! Just try to keep sane! And then, you see, if you've got your sanity, when your children are gone, you can get saved! But what are you going to do if you've lost your sanity trying to be holy? Well, is it alright to talk like this? Because the Christian life, after all, is **most ordinary**.

Let me read to you again some words that Paul wrote:

"That I may be cheered by news of you…
    genuinely anxious for your welfare…
        as soon as I see how it will go with me…
            minister to my need…
                longing for you all…
            distressed…
        he was ill…
    lest I should have sorrow upon sorrow…
that I may be less anxious…"

Oh, do you hear that? This is the same man who, in the same book said, "Have no anxiety about anything but in everything by prayer and supplication let your requests be made known unto God and the peace of God that passes understanding shall keep your hearts and minds in Christ Jesus" (Phil. 4:6-7).

Amen! That's a great text, isn't it? But the same fella wrote, "When this thing's over and everything is settled, I sure will be a lot less anxious!" And I read that and say, "Thank you brother! Thank you for this!" You see, what I sense in here is a marvelous freedom to be and to feel, and to come and to go.…

Well, you've probably guessed what my second point is. The Christian life, after all, is **most extraordinary**! And in this passage, I find two reasons. The first one is this, **Jesus is Lord of the ordinary life**.

Three times in this passage Paul uses that phrase, "In the Lord." And it fascinates me that he uses the phrase in connection with non-spiritual, ordinary kinds of things. He says, "I hope in the Lord to send Timothy to you." *I understand the sending and all this business, you know, the missionary journeys. Paul is sending his helpers here and there.* "I hope in the Lord," *now where does that "in the Lord," come in?* "I trust in the Lord that I myself shall come also." "When Epaphroditus comes, receive him in the Lord," *whatever that means.* But what I see is the opening up of

> the comings and
>> the goings,
>>> the uncertainties,
>>> the dreams,
>>>> the plans,

to the Lordship of Jesus. And I learn in this that **Jesus is Lord of the ordinary life**! But here's the point—the ordinary life does not thereby become extraordinary! But Jesus is Lord of ordinary life and THAT is **most extraordinary**!

Do you want to think about that awhile? *That lets you know we're gonna.* Jesus is Lord of ordinary which does NOT thereby cease to be ordinary. I'm not sure where it is we got the idea that if we open our lives to Christ, then wondrous and extraordinary things will follow us around or precede us wherever we go. I just need to tell you that if you give your kitchen sink to Jesus, glory will not flood the place. If you offer your desk, your workplace, your workbench, your circumstances to God and give them to him and open them up to him, they will NOT be suffused with heavenly radiance!

I just have on my heart, these days, months, maybe years of my life an awareness that the meaning of the Christian life is not to be found in escape **out of**, but in the opening up of our lives for God to come down **into**. And I think we've been programmed by miracle workers and prayer warriors and praise-the-Lord-ers to such a degree that we feel that if we really are what God wants us to be, SOMEHOW the ordinary life will be filled with glory. But oh my, if you have a headache, do you want to guess where it's going to hurt? And if someone has hurt you and disappointed you, you know where it's going to hurt! *Anybody got any Pepto-Bismol?* That's where it hurts, that's what it does to you!

And when you sorrow, you sorrow, and when you cry, you cry, and when you're glad, you're glad, and Jesus is Lord. Amen! And THAT is **most extraordinary**!

I talked to a friend of mine one time who was very sick and he said, "You know, the trouble is not just that I'm sick, but the trouble is that I don't have the feeling that I'm being as victorious as a Christian ought to be in the midst of it." Oh my! That's TERRIBLE! I mean, he not only had to be sick, he not only had to miss work, he not only had to be in pain, he had the intolerable burden of being radiant! And I wanted to give him the precious gift of praising and griping, and moaning and thanking, and acting childish and being mature, with his weight down on the love and the grace of God, in the knowledge that Jesus is Lord on

> lousy,
>> bum,
>>> awful,
>>>> no-good days,

which, unfortunately, continued to be

>>> lousy,
>> bum,

awful,

no-good days.

But Jesus is Lord! **THAT'S extraordinary**!

Here's the other reason why ordinary Christian living is most extraordinary. It's because **Jesus is identified with us in our ordinary caring for one another**. There are two marvelous passages in these paragraphs, one about Timothy and one about Epaphroditus. You remember when I read earlier something like this, "But Timothy's worth you know, how as a son with a father he has served with me in the gospel. I have no one like him. Everybody cares about their own things, not the things of Jesus Christ."

"But Timothy's worth you know. He's different, he really cares about you!" You see that? But look at it, "Timothy's not like other folks, he's a special kind of person. Everybody cares about their own thing, they don't care about the things of Christ, but Timothy is different, he CARES about you!"

If you didn't know any better, you'd say that caring about the things of Jesus Christ equals caring about YOU! Do you believe that? *No, we don't believe that, yeah we do, no we don't.* Wouldn't it be wonderful if we really did?

Then down at the bottom of the second paragraph Paul talks about Epaphroditus. Now here's the story: Paul's in prison, the Philippian church has been out of touch with him for a while, but they hear about him and they take up an offering and they put together a "care package," and they send it by Epaphroditus. So, what he's doing is bringing the care package, and he comes to the prison where Paul is and somewhere in there, he gets sick, and he nearly dies. Thank God he doesn't die! Paul said, "I'd have sorrow upon sorrow if he died, I sure am glad he didn't die, but you need to honor such men because he risked his life, for Christ!" What was he doing? Well, he was bringing a care package. We don't normally put those things together, do we, bringing a care package to someone and risking our life for Christ? Let's bring that home.

Mrs. Johnson has a whole bunch of kids, her husband gets drunk, shoots up the place. *He really did!* It's a terrible mess; she loses about everything. Mrs. Presley finds out about it and she says, "Wait a minute, that's terrible!" So, she gathers around the troops, you know, talks to all the church folks, gets some groceries, gets some clothes, gets some money, puts together a big old care package, puts it in her car and heads off for Mrs. Johnson's place and on the way has a terrible wreck. It was awful. She ended up in the hospital, thought she was going to die, but, thank the Lord, she didn't die, she's going to be OK, praise God!

How would you describe that? If you were talking about that, what would you say? I know exactly what Paul would say, "She risked her life for CHRIST!" What was she doing? Taking a care package. Isn't it amazing how Paul just takes words and just turns them around and brings things together like that? Timothy cares about Jesus. How does he do that? He's anxious for your welfare. Epaphroditus risked his life for CHRIST, bringing a care package to Paul. Folks, that's **most extraordinary**, isn't it? That Christ identifies with us not only in the great spiritual things but in the ordinary comings and goings of our lives when we open up to his Lordship.

Well, you know and so do I that there are plenty of people around
this place who
    make calls and
        write letters and
            see about things and
                handle things and
                    set up things and then
                        un-set them and then
                            re-set them
and take care of them over and over again. And I hope they know
that Jesus is present and identified with them in the loving and the
caring and the giving. I hope we haven't forgotten that Jesus said,
"In as much as you've done it unto the least of these, you have done
it unto me" (Matt. 25:45). This awesome identification of Jesus with
us at the point of
    sickness and
        uncertainty,
            insecurity and
                vulnerability, in
                    travel and
                      caring,
Jesus is present, and that is **most extraordinary**!

Well, it's time for me to tell you who I'm talking to, besides me. I
wonder if I'm talking to anyone today who really wants a miracle.
You really need a miracle. Anybody here like that? I wonder if I'm
talking to anybody who is saying,
"Oh Lord, will you,
won't you,
why don't you,
oh please, when are you?

You know I need,

oh Lord, please, Lord,

won't you, Lord?"

Now, I've just demonstrated to you my profound problem with the phrase, "*Expect a Miracle.*" See what mode that puts you in? "Have I believed enough? Can you? Won't you, please." I've come to believe that our quest for the unusual, the miraculous, the whatever it is we ought to be experiencing if we're all that God wants us to be, puts us in a kind of posture toward God that makes it very difficult for him just to come to us with his peace, with his presence. That makes it very difficult for him to enter into our lives in wondrous ways, in ordinary ways.

So, just today, I want you to bow your heads with me and do something. I'd like to ask you just to visualize your ordinary life, and I know that some of us didn't come here to do that, but I wish you would just go ahead and visualize your ordinary life. Would you do that? You know what I mean, just go ahead and look it over. And let me ask you this morning to do this: **don't expect a miracle.** It won't happen, give it up, let it go. Now we're talking just this morning, alright, right now. Just give it up.

Some of us are saying, "Oh God, change something, get me out, make it different, do something!" And this morning I'd like to ask you to just not say that. Just let it be. *That's Mother Mary's good word today, just "Let it Be."* And instead of, this morning, asking for anything, would you just open it up and let Jesus come all the way down and be Lord of it, just the way it is?

And when I talk like this, I get the feeling that if he really is Lord of it, then it can be what it is. And if I need special grace, he's there.

And if he wants to do a miracle, I guess he can. But we don't have to live with this sense of, "Won't you? Please!" or "What's the matter with me?" But we can let life be the way it is with his grace and with his love and under his Lordship.

As we sit together, would you just listen to these words of the song the choir is going to sing? And I'd like to ask you again, is there anybody here who just needs to come and lay their ordinary life before the Lord? Would this be a good place to do that? Maybe the Lord is saying to you, "Instead of asking to get out, out, out, just open it up for me to come, in, in, in." For he is Lord of ordinary life, which does not thereby cease to be ordinary, but is brought under his Lordship, and that is **most extraordinary**! Amen!

"He Giveth More Grace"
Words: Annie Johnson Flint
Music: Hubert Mitchell

Sermon #7
Who Are You Talking To?
Genesis 3 and Various Scriptures

These last four sermons were preached to, and intended for, college audiences. This is a mashup of two chapel talks, both from the early '90s. One was delivered at Point Loma College and the other at Malone College in Canton, Ohio, where Scott and I were teaching. It's clear that he's talking to college students, but the message speaks to all of us.

I want to talk to you about a question that has been going around in my mind. And the question is, **"Who are you talking to?"** If you have your Bibles, I wish you'd open them up with me to the first chapter of Genesis.

Genesis 1:1-3

[1] In the beginning God created the heavens and the earth. [2] The earth was without form and void, and darkness was upon the face of the deep; and the Spirit of God was moving over the face of the waters.

³ And God said, "Let there be light"; and there was light.

Now let's go over to the Gospel of John, chapter 1:1-4

¹ In the beginning was the Word, and the Word was with God, and the Word was God. ² He was in the beginning with God; ³ all things were made through him, and without him was not anything made that was made. ⁴ In him was life, and the life was the light of men. The light shines in the darkness and the darkness has not overcome it.

Now down to verse 14,

And the Word become flesh and dwelt among us, full of grace and truth.

Now let's go over to almost the last verse in the Bible, somewhere in the last part of in the book of Revelation 22:17,

The Spirit and the Bride say, "Come." And let him who hears say, "Come." And let him who is thirsty come, let him who desires take the water of life without price.

In the beginning, God **said**. Do you know how God creates the world? He speaks the world into being. That puts God face to face with, in the presence of, in dialogue with his creation. And when God creates man, he speaks to the human creature and enters into dialogue with him. And at the end, the Spirit and Bride say "Come." *I get the feeling that something is being said.* And I've thought about it this way, the theology of the Bible—I've come to believe this—the theology of the Bible is a theology of the word, all the way through. God takes the initiative, moves into the arena of the human situation, and speaks.

That word is a revelation; it's also an invitation. It calls for response. And I know there are many ways to talk about the relationship between God and man and the relationship between God and the world, but I really have become interested in this: the whole business can be put in terms of conversation, in terms of dialogue. And from the beginning when God **says**, to the very end when the Spirit and Bride **say**, all the way through, God is entering into dialogue, speaking to, inviting response out of which comes the cultivation of relationship.

So, God created the human creature and entered into relationship with him. Then God created the woman, and the man and the woman entered into relationship with each other, and God blessed them. And God entered into an I-thou relationship with them.

Are you familiar with I-thou? Well let me tell you about it. I-thou is a phrase that has come into our language through Martin Buber, the Jewish theologian/philosopher, and it's used as over against I-it, and it speaks to our tendency to objectify.

Let me illustrate this way: Let's go down to, I don't know, Denny's. So here we are, you know, sitting around Denny's and we put some tables together and nothing's happening, I mean, nobody comes to wait on us. And we look at each other and finally, a distracted, morose, preoccupied waitress shows up and kind of plops down paper napkins, and drops the silverware, and spills a little bit of the water, *and our minimal tip is diminishing in our minds.* And we're looking at each other saying, "What's with her?" and then someone in the group says, "How are you?" or "What's happening?" And it just pulls a cork out of the bottle and suddenly it just begins to pour out that she's a single mother,

> she has a little boy who's really sick,

> > she tried every way in the world to get off work but
> > she couldn't get off work

> > so she has to trust the neighbor to take care of him,
> maybe to take him to the hospital,

and the atmosphere in **this** room has changed, hasn't it? What's happened? We've moved from waitress-customer to hurting mother-caring people. That's I-thou. Not customer-waitress but person-person. And it isn't enough to add on a little tip *or leave a tract and be a blessing*. No, you have to say, "We sure will be praying for you," but that's not quite enough. Somebody says, "Anything we can do to help?" And you have entered into I-thou. You know how it begins? With conversation!

What I've come to understand profoundly is that God enters into I-thou relationship with his creatures! The I-thou between God and his creatures is reflected in the I-thou of the creatures. Suzanne De Dietrich says, "Paradise is a condition of transparency; God can see through his creatures, and they can see through each other." That's paradise.

Now, let me read you a story, Genesis chapter 3. Do you remember, God had placed the man in the garden and given him everything to till the garden and take care of it, and he said, "You may have of everything in the garden except you shall not eat of the tree of the knowledge of good and evil"? So, let's look at chapter 3:1-7

> Now the serpent was more subtle than any other wild creature that the LORD God had made. He said to the woman, "Did God say, 'You shall not eat of any tree of the garden'?" [2] And the woman said to the serpent, "We may eat of the fruit of the

trees of the garden; ³ but God said, 'You shall not eat of the fruit of the tree which is in the midst of the garden, neither shall you touch it, lest you die.'" ⁴ But the serpent said to the woman, "You will not die. ⁵ For God knows that when you eat of it your eyes will be opened, and you will be like God, knowing good and evil." ⁶ So when the woman saw that the tree was good for food, and that it was a delight to the eyes, and that the tree was to be desired to make one wise, she took of its fruit and ate; and she also gave some to her husband, and he ate. ⁷ Then the eyes of both were opened, and they knew that they were naked; and they sewed fig leaves together and made themselves aprons.

Oh, I hope those fig leaves were not as scratchy as the ones I know about, or else the punishment of sin had already begun!

Well, enter the serpent. So, the serpent comes and says to Eve, "Has God really said?" Look what you have, I-thou, God and his creatures in intimacy and fellowship and openness. But the serpent enters and here's the mental image I have: the three of them, the human couple and the serpent, go off out here and have a conversation about God. Did you know that original sin took place in the context of a theological discussion? That's pitiful! But it did, didn't it? There was openness **to** God, but now they go off and have a conversation **about** God in which God doesn't come off looking too good, does he?

¹ See, the serpent says, "God knows that if you eat of this, then you'll be like him, so evidently his insecurity won't tolerate your competition, and there is a hidden agenda here." And Eve thinks, "What's going on here?"

And in the context of discussion **about** God, Eve makes a decision. *I want to make that clear because once in a while we need to make clear who it is that's responsible for all our troubles! One lonely male was clapping back there!*

Do you see that? And she makes a decision that breaks the dialogue. And do you know what happens next? The openness between the two creatures is disrupted. And Adam, *the coward,* says, "The women thou gavest me…" Isn't it weird, when Adam first sees Eve he says, "Now we're getting somewhere! Bone of my bones and flesh of my flesh!" But do you know what he says now? "The woman thou gavest me…"

And it is out here in the context of talk **about** God, the covenant command is broken, the I-thou relationship is distorted. So, the parents quarrel, the children murder, and the ground is cursed. And in those first eleven chapters of Genesis, you have the awful crescendo of evil that ends up in the tower of Babel with total worldwide alienation and estrangement and hostility, defensiveness, non-communication.

Well, I know it's a little late in history, but I finally found out what Eve should have done. *That's no small insignificant item, actually,* and *I regret that this great discernment will probably not be retroactive,* but I found out what Eve should have done.

The human couple in dialogue with God—they go off out here and have a conversation, "Oh, there's some hidden agenda going on here. There's some arbitrary prohibitions going on here. Now wait a minute!" Now in this context of talking **about** God, a destructive decision is made. *Well, that's the understatement of the year!*

You know what she should have done? She should have gone back to God and said to him,

> "God, did you hear what he said?
>> You said we can do this and this, but we can't do this,
>>> and if we do this we'll die.
>>>> And he says it's because you've got a hidden agenda.
>>>> He says it's because you know that if we do, then we'll be like you—
>>> now what's going on here?
>> What's happening?"

I wish Eve would have done that.

I think I want to say to you today, there's a lot of difference between talking **to** God and talking **about** God.

I wish Eve had done what Abraham did. You remember when God called Abraham, he was already old. I mean we're talking **old**. His wife was old. And God made them a promise of

> a great nation,
>> a great family,
>>> a great name,
>>>> blessing and land.

The years went by, no child. Abraham was getting ancient, and Sarah's clock had quit ticking. And Abraham went back to God and said, "Lord, you made a promise, but it isn't coming true, what's going on?" And the conversation kept going. And that's when God appeared to Abraham in that marvelous, awesome, weird chapter 15 where God binds himself with covenant curse to be faithful to his people. What a story! I wish Eve had done that!

I wish Eve had done what Moses did. You remember when God appeared to him on the back slopes of Mt. Horeb and said, "Go down and tell old Pharoah, 'Let my people go'"? And Moses came back to God in incredible dialogue. The first thing he said was, "Who am I?" and I think the Lord said something like, "It doesn't really matter, I'll be with you." The next thing he said was, "Who are you?" And God said, "Well, I am who I am, I'm here, I'll be with you, I can handle this." Then Moses said, "They won't believe me." God said, "Well, what's that in your hand?" Then Moses said, "Well, I stutter." And God said, "I don't care, just go on down there!" And then Moses said, "Send somebody else." And God said, "Moses, that's about enough, take Aaron and go," and the dialogue kept on going. Oh, I wish Eve had done that!

And I won't even get into the great dialogue of Exodus 34 and 35 when Moses just talks to God and says, "Lord, you said you'd go with us! You can't leave us here! And don't forget, God, the neighbors are looking on and what are they going to think!" And the conversation kept going.

I wish Eve had done what David did at a time of incredible guilt and sin. I mean we're talking lust and adultery and murder, but what did he do? He came back to the God, against whom ultimately, he had sinned and said, "Have mercy on me O Lord, according to thy lovingkindness, according to the multitude of thy tender mercies, blot out my transgressions." And the conversation kept going. I wish Eve had done that.

I wish Eve had done what Jeremiah did. You remember that God called Jeremiah to go to a people and say to them what he didn't want to say, and when they heard it they didn't want to hear it, and so they persecuted Jeremiah, *and it was really like hitting the postman for bringing bad news.* He didn't want to give it, didn't want to say it, didn't want to be called. Do you know what he said over and over again to God? "God, why did you do this to me? This isn't fair." In one place he said, "You tricked me!" And the conversation kept going. The dialogue continued.

I wish Eve had done what the Psalmists did. I think about the psalms of lament. Those are the ones that say,

"O God, where were you when I needed you?

How come you didn't hear me?

My bones are out of joint,

my body's turned to water,

all the bad guys are doing good,

and the good guys are doing bad,

and you don't even care!"

There are a lot of those Psalms. Did you know that they're about two to one over the praise Psalms? But you know what the Psalmists did? They brought their complaints to God. I wish Eve had come back before she made such an awful decision, come to the God who had made the impossible demands, and kept the conversation going.

I wish Eve had done what Jesus did when in the God-forsakenness of the cross, he cried out, "My God, my God why have YOU forsaken me?" Folks, I'm here to tell you that there's all the difference in the world between, "Why have YOU forsaken me?" and saying, "How come HE has forsaken me?"

Now the question I have on my heart today is, **"Who are you talking to?"**

You know and so do I that one of the best things that goes on around a college campus is late night times to talk. You know, you get around the dormitory and, bless my soul, you solve all the problems of God, man, and the universe, and you stir up a few that haven't been thought of yet. Who hasn't been involved in this kind of stuff?

The only advice I have is that when it gets past midnight, give it up! God has the good judgment to go to bed at midnight and you would do well to follow his divine example. I have no confidence in prayers that are prayed or insights that are gained, or decisions that are made after midnight, give it up. But up until midnight, you talk.

And we all know what can happen in those sessions. We get together and talk about it and build a case and come to a conclusion... And somebody says, "Well, yeah, yeah, and what about this and what about that." And somebody says, "Well, if that's the way it is!" So, you hassle all this thing out, and somebody comes to a decision in their mind,

"Well, if that's the way it is, then there's no place in there for me!"

"I mean, if that's the way God is," or

"That's the way the church is," or

"That's what religion is, then..."

And a decision is made,

a little lever is pushed,

a little corner is turned,

a little door is closed,

and there are people precious to me who've lost their way because they made their decisions in dialogue with their peers, gathered around those with like, precious, un-faith, in discussion with like skeptical minds.

And God knows we need to talk, we need to hammer out things with each other, and if there's any loss of that, I grieve the loss of intelligent dialogue between students about real issues. That's how you sharpen your vocabulary and your wits and your thinking processes, hammering out things with each other. God help us, we need that! But before you make your decision about God, you need to come back to God and open it up to him. **Who are you talking to?**

Am I talking to anybody who's talking to all your friends about everything but not talking to God?

I'm talking to some of you who are right where Eve was. Life is great but in the middle of it, there is an irrational, arbitrary prohibition. "Keep your hands off," you say. And you're angry, and you're thinking, "Well if that's the way God is…." And you're talking to everybody but God. And God's the one you're mad at.

I'm talking to some of you who are right where Abraham was. You got a promise, you saw a vision, you had a dream, but nothing is happening, and it isn't going right and time's marching on, and you're talking to everybody else but God!

I'm talking to some of you who are right where Moses was. God has given you an impossible task and you don't think you can do it, and you don't know for sure who you are or who he is, and you wish he'd send somebody else. And I wish you'd come and talk to him about it.

My conviction today is that there are some of us here today who know the meaning of real, genuine, bona fide guilt. And maybe you're not talking to anybody. And down in the depths of your heart is silence. And you've quit talking, stopped the conversation, broken the dialogue.

And some are where Jesus was, totally forsaken and alone. Are you saying to those around you, "Why has HE forsaken me?" And you need to be saying, "Why have YOU forsaken me?"

You know what the gospel is? All the while we're trying to stop the conversation, God is trying to start it up again. He's the one who finally, in the fullness of time, speaks the Word that lives among us. And the last word in the Book of God is, "The Spirit and Bride say come, come."

I've discovered in the Bible that people can say all kinds of things to God. Some of them are terrible things! But the conversation is NEVER BROKEN because of what we say to God! In fact, what if, the awfullest, worstest, unforgivablist, terriblist sin of all is to just stop talking to God? Whatever you have to say, when you open it to God, the conversation keeps going. **Who are you talking to?**

You know, the wonderful thing about all of this is that God never ever stops speaking to us. Amen! Can you believe that? God never closes off the dialogue! And I'm talking to some of you who are in a time of
> decision or
>> loss or
>>> hurt or
>>>> guilt or
>>>>> anger.

Are you talking to everybody but God? Is there silence in the depths of your heart? If so, I pray that this will be a day that you'll begin to talk. I don't know what to say—I'm not sure that's really the point— but some of us this morning have hungry hearts and need to begin to talk.

If I could give you a precious gift, it would be the gift of knowing that the everlasting arms are underneath you all the while you're asking, "God where are you?" That the ear of God is open to you all the while you're asking, "Don't you care? Don't you hear?" The love of God surrounds you. **Who are you talking to?**

"Psalm 5 (Give Ear to My Words, O Lord)"
Words and Music: John Michael Talbot

"What a Friend We Have in Jesus"
Words: Joseph M. Scriven
Music: Charles Crozat Converse

Sermon #8
A Death to Be Died

Romans 6

⸎

This is #3 of seven messages from Romans given during the fall 1980 revival at Point Loma College (now Point Loma Nazarene University). Dad was the chaplain but, contrary to the usual pattern, was asked to preach the revival that year. Bob and Becky Harrison led the singing and provided the special music for the week. Dad includes some great review of the first two messages (and he loves review!). He mentions an alcoholic who "died" to his addiction, which is certainly possible but also reflects earlier assumptions about the nature of addiction.

There is a paragraph in the 6th chapter of Romans that I'd like to read. Romans 6:1-11

> [1] What shall we say then? Are we to continue in sin that grace may abound? [2] By no means! How can we who died to sin still live in it? [3] Do you not know that all of us who have been baptized into Christ Jesus were baptized into his death? [4] We were buried therefore with him by baptism into death, so that as Christ was raised from the dead by the glory of the Father, we too might walk in newness of life.

⁵ For if we have been united with him in a death like his, we shall certainly be united with him in a resurrection like his. ⁶ We know that our old self was crucified with him so that the sinful body might be destroyed, and we might no longer be enslaved to sin. ⁷ For he who has died is freed from sin. ⁸ But if we have died with Christ, we believe that we shall also live with him. ⁹ For we know that Christ being raised from the dead will never die again; death no longer has dominion over him. ¹⁰ The death he died he died to sin, once for all, but the life he lives he lives to God. ¹¹ So you also must consider yourselves dead to sin and alive to God in Christ Jesus.

Isn't that a great passage? Let's pray about it for just a minute before we talk about it: Our Father, in these moments that are ours together, we pray that thy word may speak to us all. I need to hear as well as speak. May my heart be open. And I pray that all of us may hear thy word. For this, we offer ourselves to thee, in thy name and for thy glory. Amen.

Well, I've been teaching long enough that I love review, and I'm having a hard time resisting the inner need to review as we've been working our way through parts of Romans. Sunday morning, we talked about, "What is the gospel?"—the gospel promised beforehand, the gospel concerning his son, the great incarnation, the resurrection of Jesus that brings us the good news of the gospel, which is God's dynamic to save!

Then Paul goes on to talk about the fundamental sin of the gentile world which, I believe, is the unwillingness to let God be God. Back in Romans 1:21a, "²¹ for although they knew God they did not honor him as God or give thanks to him," and from that follows all the estrangement, the hostility, the degradation, the darkness, that monstrous reversal that is so destructive in our lives and in our world. It's true, isn't it, when God goes off the throne there is no vacuum, self goes on the throne and that's the monstrous inversion that turns all of life awry!

Then Paul talks about the sin of the Jews, the sins of the good guys, and comes to the conclusion that there is NO distinction, all have sinned and fall short of the glory of God. And it is in full awareness of the reality of our human sinfulness that Paul declares the gracious doctrine of justification by faith. I love this quote, *I'm not sure where I got it but it's so good, I'm sure it's not mine.*

> Justification by faith is not our hopeless struggle to achieve the impossible task of pleasing God, it's accepting just as we are the offer of his love, in the confidence that instead of pouring out vials of outraged holiness, God pours out healing waters of forgiving love and treats the sinner as though he had never been away.

Amen! I wished I hadn't preached about that the other night! I'd love to preach about that again!

Folks, it is a great thing to be justified! To be put right! God declares the sinner righteous and in that declaration of God is a new creation. God brings us into right relationship with himself and that's his doing.

Another way of looking at the same thing is to see it in terms of reconciliation. See, it's just a change of dynamic. It moves us more into the realm of personal relationships, of family, of the intimacy of fellowship which God intends for us.

God does not offer us the forgiveness of the cross AFTER we come to him in contrition and remorse. Did you know that your tears do not turn on God's sympathy? Did you know that? Did you know that your loud prayers and regret and self-hate don't melt the stony heart of God? Too late, too late, he has already come, Christ has already died, while we were yet sinners, while we were enemies CHRIST. DIED. FOR. US! In our estrangement, in our hostility... Sometimes we think God won't forgive us if we didn't sin accidentally. You know what I mean? You know, when you do it deliberately, that's different...*not too, just a little bit.*

The marvelous truth is that into our defensiveness, our excuses, into all the rationalizings we build up around ourselves, God breaks through and says to us at infinite cost, "I love you; I love you," and receives us into his fellowship. Praise the Lord!

Now I wish I hadn't preached on that this morning! Isn't that great stuff? Praise God! What a wonderful thing! You see, when God moves in, he takes the initiative and that makes our repentance NOT crushing self-humiliation, but makes it possible for us to forget ourselves in openness and response to him, and we don't have to hate ourselves! Isn't that great?

Will you understand me when I say, God is not blessed by having us crawl to him hating ourselves! He doesn't want us to think less of ourselves! He wants us to think of ourselves not at all! To forget ourselves in response to him and his love! And to stop the cycle of defensiveness and self-centeredness, which rather leads us to what we're going to talk about today.

It's interesting to me, Paul has talked about the sin of the gentiles, the sin of the Jews, and has come to the conclusion that ALL have sinned and fall short of the glory of God. He has talked about justification by faith, talked about reconciliation through his blood, and then comes to a fascinating transition, seems to me, in Romans 6. "What shall we say then?"

That's interesting to me! And what I believe is that right here Paul begins to turn this coin over and talk about sanctification. And I believe that in Romans 6, 7, and 8, that's what Paul talks about. Another way to look at that would be, in Romans 6, 7, and 8, he begins to draw out the implications of what he's talked about in 3, 4, and 5. And I want to talk about that.

Here's what I believe, both the Bible and thoughtful reflection on human experience reveal a tenacious, persistent ego-centeredness in us. It's as old as Adam and deep as the well-springs of life itself. And I believe Paul reflects this in Romans 6, 7, and 8, and I see it in what I discover as a new vocabulary. In Romans 1, there is a vocabulary of sin, in Romans 2, there is a vocabulary of sin, but a different kind of vocabulary emerges in Romans 6, 7, and 8—listen to these new words:

> our old self
> > sinful body
> > > enslaved to sin
> > > > slaves of sin
> > > > > sold under sin
> > > > > > I am carnal
> > > > > > > sin which dwells in me
> > > > > > > > body of sin
> > > > > > > > > law of sin and death
> > > > > > > > > > body of death

Do you hear these words? What is Paul doing here? I believe he is dropping down to new and deeper levels and talking about an inner conflict in the heart of the justified person, and a conflict fully understood by anyone who has thought seriously about the inner life. And I believe that Paul sees the source of this inner life as the continuity of that fundamental unwillingness to let God be God. Or we could say, fundamental **self-sovereignty**, or the will to autonomy. That's a neat theological phrase. You know what automation is: self-action, self-direction. The fundamental will to autonomy, that is, our fundamental mood, posture, desire to control and govern ourselves.

I understand Paul to teach that this **old self life**, the self, centered in itself, as the source of the tension and stress. I said a while ago that anyone who has thought seriously about the inner life understands the duality and tension within.

A long time ago I read a quote from Tagore, an Indian poet. [This is from his poem "Gatanjali."] Listen to what he said:

> I came out alone on my way to my tryst,
> But who is this that follows me in the silent dark?
> I move aside to avoid his presence but I escape him not.
> He makes the dust rise from the earth with his swagger;
> He adds his loud voice to every word that I utter.
> He is my own little self, my lord,
> He knows no shame;
> But I am ashamed to come to thy door in his company.

Do you understand that? Well, let me rephrase that: I don't understand it but, yes, I do! Something in me says "yes" to that.

The late Samuel Hofenstein said,

> Everywhere I go, I go too
> And that spoils it all!

Yes!

Oh, I have to tell you a story that I love so much. A long time ago, when we were up in Pasadena, Dr. Paul Tournier made an American tour and spoke in a church in downtown Pasadena. And Mary Jo and I had been reading some of his books. He was a Christian, Swiss, psychologist and writer. He had written all kinds of good books, each one of which was better than the last. And we had read stuff like *The Meaning of Persons, Guilt and Grace,* and *The Whole Person in a Broken World,* and we had been immensely helped by his insights. So, we went down to hear him. And I never will forget it.

He told a story about one of his patients who had a dream. She and Dr. Tournier were walking down the corridor of a hospital. Both were well-dressed, as if to go to church. And as they were walking, he turned and looked at her and he noticed that she had a large nail protruding from the side of her head. She had fixed her hair to cover it up and had nearly succeeded. She didn't want anyone to see it; it was her nail. She knew she had it, she knew it had to come out, but she didn't want him to touch it because she knew that somehow, it was connected to Her. Vital. Life. Tournier's conclusion: everyone has a nail.

I have heard few things in my life that have been so expressive of the reality of our human condition! Folks, what is discordant or absurd or out of harmony on the outside is somehow connected to Our.

Vital. Life! What's fundamentally the matter with us is not just OUT HERE! It is inside.

Now A.W. Tozer picks up on that same theme and uses the biblical phrase, "the veil on the heart." And he speaks of it as the veil of our fleshly, fallen nature, living on unjudged within us, uncrucified, unrepudiated. And the closely woven threads of this veil, of which we are ashamed, which we have never truly acknowledged, which we have never brought to the cross, the threads of this veil are the hyphenated sins of the spirit, not just what we do but what we are and how we think and feel:

    self-righteousness,

       self-pity,

          self-confidence,

            self-sufficiency,

              self-love,

                self-indulgence,

and a host of others like them that manifest themselves in the

               egotism, the

            exhibitionism, the

        self-promotion, the

      hurt feelings, the

    pettiness, the

  politics

and all kinds of stuff that is so strangely at home in our religious meetings. *Well, that's enough talk about that, I guess.*

What's the matter with us is something more than what we have done, it is what we ARE, it is our fundamental posture, our fundamental attitude. It is something IN us.

Well, what is Paul's answer? I tell you, the answer is as radical as the need. And here's what I hear from this passage. Paul would say to us, "Go to the cross with Jesus and die!"

I both want and don't want to talk about this. It's easy for people like me to talk about it in ways that don't really get down and get hold of myself, but this is for us. **Go to the cross with Jesus and die!**

Another way of looking at this—I read in a book by Everett Cattell called *The Spirit of Holiness*, he illustrated it this way: take a piece of paper and put steel filings on top of it, *I'm about to tell you a little more than I know about physics,* put a magnet underneath it, and the filings will form two patterns, one around each pole of the magnet. If ever the filings are to become one harmonious pattern, one of the old patterns must cease. One of the underlying powers must be withdrawn.

Folks, there is a dying to be done. "Reckon yourselves [consider yourselves] dead to sin and alive to God in Christ Jesus." This is the call of God to us.

The question I want to talk about a little bit is, what does it mean to die?

I remember reading not long ago in one of Thomas Merton's books, "we are so accustomed to our false selves and living our false world that most of us will never know who we really are until we are dead." I've thought about that.

What I see and believe is that the call of God to us is a kind of dying before death that leads to a quality of resurrection life before resurrection. I believe that! Let me run that by again. **The call**

of God to us is a kind of death we die before we're dead that leads to a quality of resurrection life before we're resurrected!

Well, what does it mean to die? It's not a beautiful subject, and I'm so old I've heard old time preachers say, "You gotta die out." Have you ever heard a preacher say you've got to die out? I've heard old timers say, "You've gotta die like a yaller dawg under the porch." *What a way to go!*

Let's say this first of all, that the death we are called to die is not the destruction of the essential self. There is no death of the ego, the central person. That's not something I have that must die, that's ME. When that goes, I'm gone! *"Please, Mr. Custer, I don't wanna go!"*

We are talking not about the death of the essential self but the death of the self, centered in itself. We are talking about the death of a pattern of life, a quality of life, the old destructive pattern of self-centeredness, the self, centered in itself and that pattern Must. Be. Broken.

Well maybe we can talk around it better than just define it. Let me just mention a couple of things, really over-simplifications, that have been helpful to me. What does it mean to die? What is the kind of death we are to die?

A long time ago I heard a story about an alcoholic, *and I really am not talking about alcoholism, this is just the vehicle.* It was the story of a fella who went through patterns in his life. You know, he'd get himself together, get his job back, get his family back together, go along awhile and then pretty soon he'd fall back into drinking again, lose the family, lose his job, go down to the bottom. And he had a faithful pastor who, over a long period of time, loved him, cared for him. When he'd get down, the pastor would help him up and strengthen him, he'd help him to get a job, etc. The man would get along pretty well and then he'd go back down again.

Well, it seemed like he was doing really well but late one night he struggled into his pastor's study and said, "Oh pastor, if I don't have a drink, I'm just gonna die!" And the poor, tired, discouraged pastor looked at him and said, "Alright then, go home and die!" And he did! He went home and he died. And the man who came on the morrow was somehow a different sort of man because the old man had died. Does that compute?

Look at it this way, then. What happens to a person who says, "I've got to have a drink or I'll just die!"? And instead of having a drink, takes the

    desires,

        the excuses,

            the hungers,

                the insecurity,

                    the rationalizing,

                        the whole business,

takes it to the cross, gives it to Jesus there, and lets it die. That kind of stuff is helpful to me.

What happens to a person who says, "I've got to have my own way or I'll just die!" But instead takes that willfulness, whatever insecurity and defensiveness it's covering, takes it to Jesus at the cross, identifies with him there and lets it die. Folks, something very wonderful happens to a person like that!

I've told you before about a friend of ours from a long time ago, who was a pretty tall guy, 6'2" or something. He was so bright it just made you sick! He was an intellectual egghead who thought he was smart and the worst of it is, he really was. *You know, I can handle smart alecks who aren't smart, but smart alecks who really are smart really do trouble me! I don't know how to handle them!* But he was so bright and he wanted to do something great for God.

Now Mary Jo, my wife, is 5'2" and this guy is 6'2" and he used to come over to our house quite a bit, and he'd talk about all the great things he was going to do for God and how he could use his brilliant mind for God. And I remember coming in the room one time and he and Mary Jo were in a dialogue, with gestures, and I came in and he was saying to her, "Don't I have a right to do what I want with my life?" And she looked up at him and just shook her head back and forth. Folks, that is something like dying.

And I want to tell you, there are a lot of us who want to do something great for God, and that is NOT the same as giving ourselves to God for him to do with us what he wants. And the call of the gospel is, **go to the cross with Jesus and die!**

See, whatever else the cross is, it is the expression of God's "NO" to sin. On the cross, the judgment of God falls upon the reality of human sin. "He who knew no sin was made sin." And at the cross, God says, "NO" to sin. And the call of God to us is to identify with Jesus on the cross and let him say "NO" to sin in us.

See, the cross is not only something out there done FOR us—oh it's that—it is also something in which WE share. And Paul uses the analogy of baptism: dying with him, buried with him, risen with him, identifying with him In. His. DEATH! CRUCIFIED with Christ, that's Paul's phrase. I think about that.

But you know what the other side of it is? The death we're called to die is not a death for death, it's death for LIFE! It is not the death of the real self, it's the death of the false self to release the real self to become what God wants us to be. There may be a kind of life this side of death, but it isn't resurrection life. You know where resurrection life is? It's on the other side of death. And the quality of life we are to live is not just the continuity of our own human strength supported by his grace, it is a NEW QUALITY OF LIFE that comes on the other side of death!

I read this somewhere:

> The peace of God that passes understanding is on the far side of a cross, on which our sick and disordered selves have submitted to radical surgery and re-creation.

I wish that had been in the Bible!—*scribal error.*

Well, it's high time to bring this home. There's a question I want to ask you; there's some things I want to say, after all this talking. I don't believe in magic, and I think that fundamentally the changes God brings about in us are generally pretty slow, at least that's my testimony. *I could use a few more miracles in my personality; haven't had very many.* But you know and so do I there is a fundamental difference in the lives of those who have gone to the cross and those who have not. This wonderful, tall young man with great potential was never willing to go to the cross, and whatever dreams he had in those beautiful years of his life, they are long gone. That's one of the sad things in our lives, knowing him and loving him as we do.

Have you gone to the cross? Let me turn this around and say it in another way. When some of us who grew up in the church first learned to testify, the first thing we'd say was, "I love the Lord with all my heart." Is that right? I remember my daughter, Susan, when she was about two, stood up in prayer meeting one night and said, "I do love the Lord." And all the old ladies of the church said, "Oh isn't that sweet!" *Well, guess what she wanted to do the next Wednesday night—a little more, a little louder.* You know the next thing she learned, "And I want to go all the way with him." Do you know those testimonies?

Here's the question I want to ask you. Will you let the Holy Spirit help you in a response? Do you intend, at any cost, to go all the way with God? Let me say that again: Do you intend, at any cost, to go all the way with God? That's a very probing question! Whatever is in us that rises up and says, "Umm, well..." What is that? Whatever it is, bring it to the cross because that's where the power of the resurrection is revealed.

Am I talking to some of you who really want to be a Christian but you're hanging onto precious things in your life, treasured habits in your life, a certain quality of lifestyle, a certain thing you're doing that you really have not exposed to the light of God? It's not my business to outline things and give lists—I'm not interested in that—but do you have a secret, precious habit? Do you have a secret relationship? Do you have it in your mind that you can go with Christ and walk with him and follow the lifestyle of this world and somehow, it's going to be OK? Do we really hear the call to the radical obedience that comes down to the question—it seems like such a simple thing. Do you intend, at any cost, to go all the way with God?

Oh, I tell you, you answer that question from the depths with a YES and that's a death, isn't it? There is a dying, but the dying we do is the death of the false self that opens our eyes to the newness that's ours in Jesus Christ! And I pray that for you and for myself. Amen!

Will we bring to the cross anything in ourselves that's not ready to say, "Lord, I am going to go through at any cost!"? Have you made up your mind to go with Christ, at any cost? That's **death**, and that's **life**! Hallelujah!

"My Jesus, I Love Thee"
Words: William R. Featherstone
Music: Adoniram J. Gordon

Sermon #9
Give Your Bod to God

Romans 12:1–2

This is #6 of the seven 1980 PLC fall revival services. Once again, there is some wonderful review of the preceding messages. He talks toward the end of this message about those who set up and tear down—this was when chapel was held in the gym. It took a tremendous amount of work to prepare that venue for chapel services and then to get it ready for classes, practices, games, etc., held in the gym later that day.

Well, it's a good day. I'm glad to be here, and I'm glad to see you. There's just something about our being together in a spirit of understanding and love that's very precious to me. Let's look back to Romans and we're going to go now to chapter 12, verses 1 and 2. You don't even need a Bible for those two, do you?

> [1] I appeal to you therefore, brethren, by the mercies of God, to present your bodies as a living sacrifice, holy and acceptable to God, which is your spiritual worship. [2] Do not be conformed to this world but be transformed by the renewal of your mind, that you may prove what is the will of God, what is good and acceptable and perfect.

There's no way for us to really understand the passage if we do not take it in the context of the rest of the epistle. You see, the passage just before this one, the end of chapter 11, closes like this:

> [33] O the depth of the riches and wisdom and knowledge of God! How unsearchable are his judgments and how inscrutable his ways!
>
> [34] "For who has known the mind of the Lord, or who has been his counselor?"
> [35] "Or who has given a gift to him that he might be repaid?"
>
> [36] For **from** him and **through** him and **to** him are all things. To him be glory forever. Amen.

Now, that passage is the climax of Romans 1-11 in which he talks about the sin of men in the first great "Therefore" in Romans 3:20, when he says, "Therefore, by the deeds of the law there shall no flesh be justified" (KJV). Then in the full awareness of the reality of our human predicament, we have the great "Therefore" of justification by faith in Romans 5:1, "Therefore, being justified by faith we have peace with God through our Lord, Jesus Christ." Then he begins to turn the coin over and talk about the deeper sin problem in our lives, our old self, carnal mind, carnal nature, body of sin, etc., etc., and comes to the marvelous conclusion in the third great "Therefore" in Romans 8:1, "There is therefore now no condemnation for those who are in Christ Jesus. For the law of the Spirit of life in Christ Jesus has set me free from the law of sin and death."

Then he goes on in Romans 9, 10 and 11 to talk about God's great providential work in history, working with the gentiles, working with the Jews to bring to fulfillment his ultimate purposes. And then the great climax in Hebrews 11, "[33] O the depth of the riches and wisdom and knowledge of God! How unsearchable are his judgments and how inscrutable his ways...[36] For **from** him and **through** him and **to** him are all things. To him be glory forever. Amen."

THEREFORE, **give your bod to God**! Just. Like. That! You know, that's typical of Paul. And it isn't simply that ethical sections follow doctrinal sections, it is that practical ethical sections come out of, and are intimately related to, the whole of what he has to say in the theological sections. In fact, the whole thing is the theology of it.

Do you know what the call of God is to you and me? **Give our bodies**! Therefore, being justified by faith.... Therefore, being free from condemnation by the indwelling power of the Spirit of Christ.... All the great spiritual blessings which God gives are to focus in on the Giving. Of. Our. Bodies. To. Him.

Did you know that the Christian believes that his body belongs to God just as much as his soul does? In fact, in the Bible, you don't have a clear dividing up of body, soul, and spirit. There is the person, the **embodied** person.

For instance, I have a body; my body is not me, but me and my body are just like **that** (fingers crossed). Now I am not a body; I have one. And if somebody starts to cut off my hand I say, "Now, don't do that, that's mine! It belongs to me! Don't do that!" I don't say, "That's me." *I have wondered at what point I would stop saying that's mine and start saying, "That's me!"* But this much is clear, when Paul uses the word, "body," he does not mean simply the physical life, he means our whole embodied selves.

That's an important idea for us. Don't divide up spirit, soul and body. Body means the whole person, here and now. The person is not the body but, (*Have you ever noticed this?*) if you want to know somebody, you have to get somewhere where their body is. You don't really know anyone if you haven't been reasonably near their body. Just think about that! *Very profound!* You know, you don't know someone by just talking to them over the phone. You certainly don't know them simply by writing letters. Anyone writing letters to people they love far away? Do you want to testify at this point? Letters communicate, but letters also miscommunicate, don't they?

I don't have time to say this but I'm going to anyhow. You know, the trouble with writing love letters is that you write them at night when you're feeling romantic and you read them at 10 o'clock in the morning! If you really want good communication, read them at 10 o'clock at night! You don't know someone just by writing, you don't know someone just by phoning. You know how you get to know someone? By getting close to them, in the body.

And for that matter, whatever we do, we do in the body. J.T. Seamans says that, "The swinging doors of our existence are our body." I like that! The body becomes the swinging door, that is, it swings in and we receive—

    looks,

        feelings,

            we see,

                we hear,

                    we sense, and

                        we receive through the five senses.

We can tell what is being implied, what is being felt, and the body becomes the source of these dynamics, the paralanguage. Then the door swings out and we

give a warm hand or a clenched fist, or
we resist or
our eyes say things,
our expressions say things.

Our body is our point of contact with our world and with other persons. That's fascinating to me.

And I've thought about this, folks, when God wanted to do the BEST THING HE EVER DID, when God wanted to do the MOST SPIRITUAL THING he could ever do to redeem us lost folk, he came in Jesus Christ in a body! Just think about that! When God wanted to save us, he didn't come as a spirit, he came in a **body**.

And then we think of the church, which is his body. See, the body is our point of contact with other persons. The body is God's point of contact with us, and the church is his body, which is his point of contact for the saving of the world! So, as Christians, then, we are not to despise the body, not to reject the body, not to indulge or worship the body, **but** to Present. Our. Bodies. A. Living. Sacrifice. That is, all that we are, all that we do every day, our ordinary work

at home and
school and
shop and
office and
field,

and offer it to God as an Act. Of. Worship! Look at the translation here, "Present your bodies as a living sacrifice, holy and acceptable to God, Which. Is. Your. **Spiritual**. **Worship**."

I have discovered a marvelous thing, and it is making a difference in my whole view toward the Christian life. It is this: our spiritual worship is the offering of our bodies to God! That's remarkable!

We have a tendency to divide up
    spiritual and secular,
        sacred and profane,
            what is worship and what is not worship,
                what is holy and what is ordinary.
But did you know that True. Real. Spiritual. Worship. is not just
                      praying or
                  singing or
              teaching a class or
           being up front or
        leading or
      doing something spiritual?
Real genuine bona fide spiritual worship is the giving to God of Our. Embodied. Selves!

It's what we do day by day. I read of a housewife who spent a considerable amount of time doing mundane things in the kitchen; she put a motto over the sink that said, "Divine Service Conducted Here Daily." That's it!

And when Paul talks about the gifts in Ephesians 4, he says, "[11] And his gifts were that some should be apostles, some prophets, some evangelists, some pastors and teachers, [12] to equip the saints for the work of ministry, for building up the body of Christ," and all the way through the New Testament, ministry means service! It means, actual, ordinary, plain stuff. And what I see in the passage is the call to give to him my body, and that giving is my spiritual worship!

I think I think that by and large, we are more spiritual than Jesus was. I believe that. I'm not saying we're more holy, but I believe we're more spiritual. We divide things up, don't we, the spiritual things. And

>the more we pray,
>>the more we get with God,
>>>the more devotions we have,
>>>>the more holy we become,
>>>>>the more we withdraw,

and the things of earth become less and less and we think someday Jesus is going to rip us all off to heaven and save us from all the troubles of the world. Amen! And we think that spiritual growth is the gradual process of withdrawal from the world. And then you go back to the words of Jesus and that theory just gets all messed up!

Do you remember the great story he told about the sheep and the goats, the great eschatological passage in Matthew's Gospel where he says all nations will gather before him, the sheep on the one hand and the goats on the other? And do you remember he says to these, "Come you blessed of my father…" and to the others, "Depart you into darkness…," that awesome passage there? Do you know what's in-between those two? Do know what's the line that makes the difference between whether you go into eternal life or eternal darkness? "I was hungry; I was thirsty; I was in prison." "Oh Lord, didn't we prophesy and do many mighty works in your name?" "Yeah, yeah, yeah, I don't know you. I was hungry, I was thirsty." I don't like to talk very much about that because it messes me up. It's a lot easier for me to be spiritual.

My student assistant made a sign for me one time that said:

I am your friendly, loving, caring chaplain
Tuesdays and Thursdays from 2-3pm

Then I turned it over on the other side and it said:

Do not disturb, being holy.

So, if you see that on my door, you see, I don't have time to hear
about your troubles,
I've got to be holy!
I've got to get away!
I've got to be spiritual!
If I'm going to be chaplain, I don't have time to
help you with your troubles!

Then, you read the words of Paul and it tears it all to pieces! Because
our spiritual worship is the offering of our daily lives to him! I praise
God for that! That means something to me. Our daily lives, what we
do with them day by day, this is our spiritual worship!

I think so often of the fact that we come here to have a spiritual
service and before the service begins, then after the service is over,
there are a bunch of fellas who work their heads off. *Well, it's not their
heads that they work off but I said "heads."* But they work them off to get
ready, do you know that? And while we're having spiritual times
afterward, they make a whole bunch of racket putting these things
back; *that's the worst noise in the whole world!* They bring them out and
then put them back, sweep up the place, roll this in, and we're all set
up to be holy. Then they have to take it all back down again, and
sometimes I wonder, are we the ones having the spiritual worship
and they're the ones doing all the work?

All around this campus, somebody has to mow the lawns and water the flowers and clean up the restrooms and sweep the floors and do all kinds of stuff, and in my heart, I wonder, "Do we know that this is what it really is?" C'mon, do we know that this is what it really is?

Have we divided up our lives in such a way that we can go off and be holy and say holy things but it doesn't have any relationship to
> how you act in the dorm or
>> how you act on a date or
>>> how fast you drive up and down these roads? Amen!
You cut it out, folks! That's your spiritual worship!

How we talk,

how we behave,

what we do in the library,

what we do in the dining hall,

how we behave in the gym and

in the locker rooms...

Do we know that our spiritual life, our worship, is not just praying and being holy, it is the OFFERING of our BODIES to GOD. THAT'S our spiritual worship!

And the remarkable thing is that as we offer him our bodies, which is our spiritual worship, we are **renewed** in our minds. That's just something else! Do you need to be renewed from the inside? Then give God your body! Sometimes I wonder if we have it all backwards. Do you want to love God? Start loving people! Do you want to have your mind cleared? Give him your body! Do you need renewal?
> Don't move away from the common, the ordinary,
>> don't move away from homework,
>>> don't move away from assignments,

don't make a distinction between the holiness of
devotions and the holiness of studying for a test!

They are NOT separate! Both of them are holy. They are not the
same, but one is not holy and the other secular. Folks, they are
TOGETHER, and we've got to learn how to make altars out of our
desks and do our assignments as unto Jesus, and write papers as a
part of our whole spiritual commitment, or WHO we are as a school,
or WHAT we are doesn't mean a THING IN THE WORLD!

Why am I yelling? Maybe I need this; maybe you need this. The
renewal of our minds! Isn't it wonderful how God remakes us
from within? The world seeks conformity, but God works from the
inside—I just love that! We just have it backwards. We think the
world sets us free and the church brings conformity. That is wrong,
folks! The world brings conformity:
What are we supposed to be eating?
What are we supposed to be brushing our teeth with?
What are we supposed to be wearing?
What are we supposed to be driving?

We hear it everywhere—there is a product, there is a way, there is a
uniform. The world has its uniform, its lifestyle, and it's all the same!
There is a conformity that brings about a bondage to the WHOLE
SYSTEM! And the awesome power of the world is that it exercises a
controlling influence on every new life born into it.

Have you ever seen 12- and 13-year-olds smoking on the sidewalk,
acting so big and grown up? Have you ever seen little junior high
girls in cocktail dresses wishing they had what it took to fill them out,
painted up, dolled up,
padded up, pouty? The destructive conformity of the world!

And then God comes to us to remake us from the inside. And do you know where it begins? Just the simple, plain, ordinary thing—give him your body! Maybe that's behind the tradition of going to the altar. Did you know that the altar is an American institution? And for 1900 years the gospel moved ahead without any such "animal." *I don't know what to do about the fact that Jesus never heard anybody sing, "Just as I Am."* But, do you know what I think? Part of the beauty of the symbolism of the altar is, when you want to do spiritual business with God, you can just get your bod there, or somewhere like it, kneel down, and offer it all to him.

Well, amen! Does anybody want to come and pray? Let's sing this wonderful hymn together:

"Take My Life and Let It Be Consecrated"
Words: Frances R. Havergal
Music: Henri A. Cesar Malan

That's a beautiful song and I like it because it takes the hunger and spiritual desire of our hearts and brings it down to its expression in our hands, our feet, our lips, how we live. If you'd like to come and pray; if God is saying something to you and you'd like to respond in the real, genuine way of just bringing your body here to give to him the whole of your life, do it while we sing.

Sermon #10
Stuff That's Great from Romans 8
Romans 8 (KJV/RSV)

~~~

This is message #7 from Romans, the one that closed the 1980 revival on Wednesday night at PLC. The morning message was from Romans 12, but he must have decided he wanted to end with the "great stuff" from chapter 8.

Thank you, Bob and Becky, and thank you, everybody. It's been a great time for me. It's a good thing it's coming to an end—I've told you all I know and quite a bit besides!

I want to talk to you again tonight from the book of Romans, and, especially tonight, I want to talk about some stuff that's great from Romans 8. Maybe it has become obvious to you that the stuff that's in Romans has become a fundamental base for my own understanding of the Christian life. And it has been a significant transition in my life to move away from my earlier understanding of what it means to be a Christian—from simply background, context, church, and what I've heard people say—over to a growing acceptance of the truth of the word of God as the base for what I believe. That has meant so much to me; I can't tell you how deeply I pray and desire that for you, too.

And I don't know just what to call what I'm going to do tonight: kind of God, Romans, and me. First, I'd like to share with you some review. *You can tell we're getting down to the close of the meeting; I'm running out of new stuff, and I have to spend more and more time reviewing—which kind of takes up the slack!*

I'd like to pick up some of the things we've been talking about and then spend a little bit of time with you tonight in the 8th chapter of Romans to talk about the great things going for us, from God, as we live life between the times.

I wish you'd open up your Bibles to Romans 8. I won't have a particular text; I'm just going to read passages out of the chapter and pick up on several of the paragraphs in it. But as I have come to understand myself and God, and his work in the world redemptively, and in me redemptively, it seems to me, the first thing that I learn from Romans is a deep acceptance of our condition under God. At one and the same time, we are in the image of God and fallen. There is our grandeur, and there is our misery. But in that stress, the stress of the human situation, is the reality of our lives. We who are made in the image of God yet fallen. And it is in full awareness of the reality of our fallenness that the gospel comes to us with a saving word.

I have to say to you that I have come to understand and appreciate more than ever in my whole life, the beauty and glory of genuine, free forgiveness, in the light of the depth and reality of human sinfulness. And the two of them go side by side. They. Are. Together! Don't think that forgiveness is shallow, or that

free forgiveness means a cheap view of sin, or that

it leads to antinomianism, or

you can do whatever you want because you're
saved,

not if you know what it means to be a sinner, not if you KNOW what
it means to be truly forgiven.

ALL have sinned and fall short of the glory of God and There. Is.
No. Distinction! But, thank God, being justified by faith, We. Have.
Peace. With. God. Do you believe that? Since all have sinned and
fall short of the glory of God, they are justified By. His. Grace. As.
A. Gift, through the redemption which is in Christ Jesus. God's
outpoured, freely given, unmerited love, on my behalf. Amen! It's a
wonderful thing to be saved!

Then what I learn from Romans is that to live in Christ means to be
brought to a wonderful breakup of the tyranny of the pattern of the
old self-life. You remember in Romans 6 we talked about the dying
motif. There is a death to be died, a death to the false pattern of the
old destructive self-life and a newness that's ours in him. Dying with
him; rising with him. I just believe with all of my heart that there
is a death for us to die before we're dead so that we may live in him
a resurrection life before the resurrection. I just happen to like that
way of thinking about it. That computes with me. And the death we
are called to die is a death to the pattern of the old destructive ways
of self-centeredness, the will to autonomy, self-sovereignty. To GO
TO THE CROSS WITH JESUS AND DIE, is to experience in the
power of his Spirit, newness of resurrection power. Praise God!

Then the life that we live in him is a life of growing, continuing yieldedness and openness to him in which we bring to the cross the new things we learn about ourselves, our failures, our discoveries, the events of our lives, and there at the cross we find manifested the power of the resurrection. Praise God!

Then it means a gracious freedom. It means freedom from legalism. Christ is the end of the law. I wish I hadn't preached about that already; I'd love to do it tonight, again! *We may spend the rest of the quarter in Romans. Roamin' through Romans with Reuben; maybe that's too much!*

Well, hear this wonderful quote from John Bunyan:
> To run and work the law commands,
> But gives us neither feet nor hands.
> But better news the gospel brings,
> It bids us fly and gives us wings.

Amen! I thank God that we live in a glorious freedom because HE. HAS. SET. US. FREE. from the FALSE patterns and the FALSE images and the bondages, to let us love and become.

More than that, he sets us free from the power of sin and death. There is no minimizing of the reality, the demonic reality of the power of evil but, thank God, there is a different, new, powerful law at work that sets us free from the law of sin and death!

> [1] There is therefore now no condemnation for those who are in Christ Jesus. [2] For the law of the Spirit of life in Christ Jesus has set me free from the law of sin and death. [3] For God has done what the law, weakened by the flesh, could not do:

sending his own Son in the likeness of sinful flesh and for sin, he condemned sin in the flesh... (Rom. 8:1-3)

Right in the arena where sin had won the victory, Christ came and accomplished a triumph in which, praise God, we may share! He has won for us the victory at the level where sin exercises control! Praise God forever! That is true liberty!

Well, I really do believe this stuff! Do you? I just believe this stuff. And what God is helping me to do in these years of my life is to put my weight down on what is here; and I find as I do, that the inner witness corresponds to the truth and my heart says, "YES"! Praise God!

Then the thing that I want to talk a little bit about now out of Romans 8 is this: as I live out life in Christ, life in the Spirit, within the context of the earthly existence that's mine, GOD. IS. FOR ME. and GOD. IS. FOR. YOU! I believe that! God is for us!

I'm impressed by a couple of things in Romans 8. One is the incredible victory that is described and experienced in it, woven in and around an incredible acceptance of the realities of our human condition.

Maybe you have been picking up from what I have been saying that I do not see salvation as taking us up and away. I see salvation as God coming down and working within. I believe that! And the older I get and the longer I am privileged to live the Christian life, the more I believe that we are not spared what it means to be human. We do not, any of us, escape the WEAKNESS and the VULNERABILITY of our humanity!

The other day a guy came into my office and talked about this girlfriend, Cathy, who was suddenly sick and in the hospital with some kind of nerve disease, and he shook his head and said something like, "That's not fair! Just last weekend we were out on the beach and having such a great time and now she's in the hospital!" And he was half confused and half angry... *Whatever other halves he has, I don't know what they're feeling, but I understand that!* Do you understand that? And here he is trusting God, trying to live the Christian life; there they are having a happy time and then BOOM, there she is in the hospital!

This story is very fresh with me but we could go back day by day and week by week and here you are, here at school, and something's happening at home, and somebody's father-in-law falls out of a tree and has all kinds of problems! He's hurt bad—and everything was going along fine and then BOOM, just like that! Folks, we are VULNERABLE! We are WEAK and we live in the human condition!

And I am having fears about, and increasing resistance against, the kind of preaching that says
> if you're really loving God and
>> if you're really obeying and
>>> paying your tithe and
>>>> really filled with the Spirit and
>>>>> walking in the light,

then doors will open and everything will go well, and success will come, everything will happen beautifully. *Oh brother!*

"Just keep those cards and letters coming in, folks! Then we can
    build our cathedral,
        we can buy our mountain,
            we can build our hospital,
                we can build our empire,
                    we can keep this program on the air!
And if you'll trust God and send in your money, God will just bless
you and you'll prosper." *And all this kind of baloney! They don't say that;
that's what I say! And I finally found out that the only way for me to keep saved
is to turn it off!*

That doesn't have to be your testimony, but it sure is my testimony.
And sometimes we get the idea that if we live for God and are filled
with the Spirit, somehow when pain comes it won't hurt, and when
we are lonely, we won't feel alone if Jesus is with us, and when failure
experiences come, we won't feel failure. And then I begin to read
again in this MARVELOUS chapter of triumph—
    our mortal bodies,
        suffering,
            inward groanings,
                our weakness,
                    tribulation,
                        distress,
                  persecution,
            famine,
          nakedness,
     peril,
  sword.

Think about is this way, the life that we live in Christ is life between
the times. That's a very helpful idea to me. I guess partly because I

can visualize it, *though I seldom use gestures, it helps me sometimes.* We are living between the times. Obviously, we're living between birth and death—*isn't that profound?* We are living between the first coming and the second coming of Jesus. Where are we in that? You know there are some people who think we are very, very close to Jesus' second coming.

I don't know if I ought to tell you this or not, but the Lord came to me not long ago and told me he's not coming back for 200 years. So, I said, "Oh, OK Lord; I didn't think you were anyhow but, I'm glad to have it confirmed." What's your problem with that? Hmm? Don't I have just as much right to say he's not coming for 200 years as you to say that he's coming day after tomorrow? Yea, I do, *especially when I'm right! Isn't it wonderful?* Well, I should tell you that just before he left, he said to me, "On the other hand, I might come tomorrow."

But I've thought about that, and as a matter of fact, I don't think he's coming for at least 200 years. You know what that means to me? I'll tell you what that means to me—if that's the way it is then I best face life the way it is. Amen! And if there are wrongs to be righted, I guess I'd best get with the program, and if there are people who are hurting that need to be helped, I guess I best not wait for Jesus to come down and rip me off to heaven and leave them behind. I guess I best be helping and loving and caring. And if there are problems to face, I better face them. If there are things unreconciled that need to be reconciled, I guess I better be getting with the program. If there are hurts that need to be healed, I suppose if there's going to be some time, I'd just as well get with the program because while I am involved in all of that, there is the gracious, sustaining, caring, loving presence of God that does not take us OUT of the world but keeps us IN this world!

And we've heard that a hundred times but somehow, we think of grace lifting us out, and that image is a gracious image, but if it means that somehow it lifts us out of the genuine stress, and the genuine hurt, and the genuine loneliness, then we've missed what it means.

You know, I've been toying in my mind whether to talk about this or not, but we have a daughter who is 30 years old who is brain damaged, has been institutionalized for most of her life, and has been in a board-and-care facility in San Diego for the last several years. She is not doing well, in fact, not doing well at all. And a couple of days before school started, we went to court. First day of school, she was transferred to Agnew's Hospital in San Jose—bad news. Just bad news.

Now, the reason I talk about it is not only what it means to me but, I just want to say to you that it is a recognition of the reality of the human situation and there are 300 testimonies right here tonight that could duplicate it in one way or another. Do you believe that? I do. There are 300 at least, 300 testimonies something like that. *Great way to start the year!*

Alright, what's the reality? That's the reality! What else is the reality?
    God's love,
        God's presence,
            God's grace.
            It doesn't mean it doesn't hurt,
        it doesn't mean you understand,
    it doesn't mean it's OK,
but it does mean the grace and mercy and presence of God when we are hurting.

Now it seems to me that in Romans 8 there are some marvelous insights about the kind of help God gives to us, the quality of victory which we may share as we live in this context.

One of the good ones that I find is in verses 14-16. Folks, living as we do in earthen vessels, limited in our knowledge and understanding, we yet have the witness of the Spirit as to our relationship with God. Amen! Isn't that a gracious thing? Take a look at it.

> [14] For all who are led by the Spirit of God are sons of God.

I memorized this in the King James and I can't really do it any other way.

> [15] For ye have not received the spirit of bondage again to fear; but ye have received the Spirit of adoption, whereby we cry, Abba, Father. [16] The Spirit itself beareth witness with our spirit, that we are the children of God: [17] And if children, then heirs; heirs of God, and joint-heirs with Christ...

Did you know that the precious gift of the Holy Spirit to us, as we live life in the stress of the human situation, is that we may yet have the assurance of our relationship with God? The word "Abba" is a wonderful word; it was Jesus' own word for his father. And the marvelous, astounding truth is that Jesus passes on to us something of the same quality of relationship he has with his father. Amen!

Did you know that at the heart and center of Jesus' life was the intimacy of his relationship with his Father? That's what gave him his

confidence, that's where he got his
assurance, that's the source of his
astounding power, that's the source of his
independence of men.

He moved with authority under a dictatorship,
he moved with confidence in a world filled with war and
stress,
he lived with assurance in the midst of doubt,
because at the heart of his life was his trust in his Father. He. Knew. Who. He. Was! And I thank God for that!

I never will forget, a long time ago, I'd been pastoring for quite a while and there was a square in a park close to the church, and I was trying to learn Romans 8. And the wonderful thing about trying to memorize something is that you have to go over it and over it and over it. And I was walking around the square early one morning trying to memorize it and I was going over this passage, "¹⁵ We have not received a spirit of bondage again to fear, we have received a spirit of adoption when we cry, Abba, Father. ¹⁶ The Spirit himself bears witness with our spirit, that we are the children of God" (Romans 8:15-16).

I will never forget the marvelous sense of assurance that came to my life! My heart was saying, "Father!" And I knew that already but somehow it broke in on me in a way that left me walking around the square saying to myself, "Hey, I'm saved! I'm saved! I really am saved!" I never will forget that!

And it means that I have the privilege of knowing who I am. In all that I don't know, the vulnerability, the weakness, the stress, all that means to live in the human situation—local and worldwide—we have the privilege of knowing Who. We. Are. Children of God with an Abba Father relationship. Amen!

Then the glory of the whole business is, that though we share the creatures' bondage to corruption, the Spirit helps us in our weakness and **interprets** our **praying**. Oh, isn't that great?

You know it has helped me to discover that it was St. Paul who wrote this verse, "We do not know what to pray for as we ought." I've always felt like that this was the testimony of us lesser Christians. Paul, himself, said that, and it's my testimony, too. We. Do. Not. Know. What. To. Pray. For. as we ought.

Have you discovered, as I have, that when you're little, you can pray little prayers for little people, but when you get big, it's harder to pray big prayers for big needs for big people? You understand that, don't you? When the children were little, we prayed, "Lord, keep them well and give them a happy day." But they aren't little anymore and somehow, those prayers just don't seem quite adequate. They're OK prayers, and, you know, I can pray,

    "Lord, bless the family,
       bless our loved ones,
          bless those who have needs,
             bless the college,
               bless the President,
             bless everybody what needs blessin', Lord!
       Bless 'em good.
    Just all the needs, you know all the needs, Lord.
   Just bless everybody!"

I had a fellow in a church one time that would say, "Give 'em a hand, Lord, give 'em a hand."

I can handle the "blessing" prayers, but when I try to articulate the real concerns of my life, and try to enter into the real concerns of

God, it becomes increasingly difficult. But the wonderful truth is, the Holy Spirit knows the mind of God and the Holy Spirit knows my heart. And I don't have to say it right because he knows what I'm getting at, and I may pour out my heart before him. And the Spirit intercedes with groanings which cannot be uttered.

It's interesting, there are three "groanings" in the passage. There is the groaning and travailing of creation, there is the groaning of the believer, and the groaning of the Spirit. It testifies to the fact that we are in-between the "already" and the "not yet." You see, we have received the gift of salvation but it is not yet consummated so, we are in the stress of what we have received and what is yet to be received. And in that stress, the blessed Holy Spirit opens up, reveals, interprets, and intercedes. Praise God, forever! It's the privilege that's ours as we live in our unknowing.

Then, thank God, though we live in a world, somebody said, "of whim and circumstance where the arrows of fate are shot at random and germs do not discriminate." Caught as we are in the tensions and determinisms of the human situation, God works in all the affairs of our lives for good!

And I want to tell you, I believe Romans 8:28, "²⁸ We know that in everything God works for good with those who love him, who are called according to his purpose."

Hallelujah! Do you believe that? I don't know anything that means more to me than this fundamental idea from Romans 8:28. Now there are some things that it doesn't mean.

You know that there are people who believe that
    everything is going to be alright, and
        the good outweighs the bad, and
            things are going to be fine;
                behind every cloud there's a silver lining, and
                  don't worry, it's going to be alright.
And there are people who praise God for everything—have you run into that idea? They just praise God for everything. I have a hard time with that because it assumes that nothing is really evil. It's a denial of the reality of evil! And evil is real. And there are no cheap and shallow answers to the evils of our world. And this verse doesn't mean that somehow, things are just going to come out OK in the end.

Romans 8:28 means more than that. Let me tell you what I believe it means. Though many things happen that are not in accordance with God's will, nothing happens that is beyond it, or outside it, that is, outside the arena where God is at work, not only in judgment but in creative, healing power. I cannot tell you how deeply I believe that! There are many things that happen that are not in accordance with God's will, oh that's true, but NOTHING, NOTHING happens that is outside, NOTHING happens that's beyond where God is at work, not only in judgment but in CREATION, in REDEMPTION, in HEALING, and RENEWAL. Folks, nothing is beyond where God is working! I believe that!

And you know, I've lived long enough, I've just about decided not to give up on anybody! I had the experience just recently of running into a whole group of people, I guess three or four or five families in the last three or four or five months that I used to know. And I met some guys who, when they were in college, weren't worth a tin horn! They were a pain in the neck, and I wished we'd kicked 'em out and I don't know why we didn't, but we didn't. And lo and behold, they are living for God, at peace, happy in the Lord, serving in the kingdom, in MINISTRY, HELPING, WORKING, SERVING! And I think, *I'm not totally convinced, but* I just don't want to give up on anybody anymore! It doesn't pay! And I believe that beyond the worst that can happen that God is still at work. Amen! That BEYOND when WORSE has come to WORST, God isn't Done. Yet. By. Any. Means. Hallelujah! I believe that! He is working and he isn't done!

Well, it's time to quit but let me just yell at you one more thing. In all of this whole business of our human situation, God is FOR us. Amen! Let's move on in that passage.

> [31] What shall we then say to these things? If God be for us, WHO can be against us?

Listen to this one.

> [32] He that spared not his own Son, but delivered HIM up for us all, how shall he not with him also Freely. Give us. All. Things?

> [33] WHO shall lay anything to the charge of God's elect? It is God that justifieth.

> [34] WHO is he that condemneth...?

> [35] WHO shall separate us...?

I love those "whos"! *A sermon for owls.*

I tell you, God's love, God's grace, God's mercy, is not a fickle, fleeting, flighty thing. God's great knowledge from before is matched by his grace choosing to redeem us, is matched by his INCREDIBLE self-giving to save us, and is fulfilled by his MARVELOUS self-giving in grace and love.

All the way along there is no break in the golden chain of the redemptive work of God who, from the time he ever knew us until the time he gets us home to heaven, Will. Never. Let. Us. Go! Hallelujah!

I don't believe once in grace always in grace. I don't believe that. I believe once in grace, **almost** always in grace. I do believe that. Will you understand me when I tell you that it is not an easy thing to backslide! It's not as easy as you think! You're not off the hook just because you decide to be rebellious or worldly for a while. Amen!

We make lousy rebels, we do, and very awkward sinners. You know, when Christian folk try to go to the devil, they do it very poorly, you know that? They aren't even suave (pronounced swave); they are awkward.

No, I tell you what I believe, the winds of God are blowing, winds of love, winds of grace, winds of providence are blowing! For me to get my sails up in those winds means to be brought safely where I want to go! Hallelujah! I just believe that!

Change that, the currents of God are flowing. GOD is at work. GOD is present in all of our lives and for me to cast MYSELF into that current is to be carried where I want to go!

Well, time to quit. Let me tell you who I'm talking to specifically right now. I wonder if I'm talking to anyone here tonight who feels like you're weak and the devil's strong and you don't even know if you're going to make it. Anybody feeling so discouraged, God's far away, you're so weak, everything is piling up, and you don't even know if you can make it?

Oh, if I could give you a precious gift, it would be the gift of transference from reliance upon your own psychic energy and your own emotional self-centeredness onto the solid truth of the word of God. It would be that the Holy Spirit would let you know that you are in his love and you are in his care. He will not let you go! He knows you from way before! His DESTINY for you is that you be conformed to the image of Christ. And ALL you need for this to take place is found in his MARVELOUS

    self-giving love and

        grace and

            mercy and

                strength and the

                    help of his Spirit.

[38] For I am persuaded, that neither death, nor life, nor angels, nor principalities, nor powers, nor things present, nor things to come,

[39] Nor height, nor depth, nor any other creature, shall be able to separate us from the love of God, which is in Christ Jesus our Lord.
(Romans 8:38-39)

Amen! I do rather like this book, you know? My old granddad used to say, "If I didn't have good religion, I'd get it!" I'm just feeling that way tonight.

I need this stuff tomorrow, you know? I need this stuff in the stress, the sorrows, the burdens, the cares, the hopes, the dreams of my life.

I need to know that I'm his child, praise God! I need to know that there's help for me when I don't know what to pray. I need to know that in all the affairs of life, God is at work, and that ultimately, There. Is. No. Separation. from the love of God which is in Christ Jesus, our Lord! Amen!

Let's sing this song together. If you want to come and pray, why don't you do it?

"The Solid Rock"
Words: Edward Mote
Music: William B. Bradbury

To Timothy and All Other Disciples
Probing Thoughts on Second Timothy

Reuben Welch

Contents

1
We Live Where We Live
2 Timothy 1:1-7

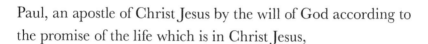

Paul, an apostle of Christ Jesus by the will of God according to the promise of the life which is in Christ Jesus,

[2] To Timothy, my beloved child:
Grace, mercy, and peace from God the Father and Christ Jesus our Lord.

[3] I thank God whom I serve with a clear conscience, as did my fathers, when I remember you constantly in my prayers. [4] As I remember your tears, I long night and day to see you, that I may be filled with joy. [5] I am reminded of your sincere faith, a faith that dwelt first in your grandmother Lois and your mother Eunice and now, I am sure, dwells in you. [6] Hence I remind you to rekindle the gift of God that is within you through the laying on of my hands; [7] for God did not give us a spirit of timidity but a spirit of power and love and self-control.

I am amazed at how much we have in common with Timothy. Like many of us, he lived in a cosmopolitan city. Ephesus was an ancient city founded in the 11th century B.C., taken by Alexander the Great in 334 B.C., and by the Romans in about 138 B.C. *I'm sure you're blessed to know that!*

What mattered for Timothy was that the Ephesus he knew still held within it elements of all the different cultures it had ever known. It was the center of culture, art, and religion. It was the home of Diana, the goddess of fertility, whose temple was one of the seven wonders of the ancient world. Larger than a football field, it was a sanctuary for the goddess of sex.

We must say that people in ancient cultures were more forthright than we are. They had a sex goddess and built her a temple and worshiped her. We wouldn't do anything like that! We just permeate our whole consumer society with sex, merchandise it through advertising, put it in all our TV programs and call it "Charlie's Angels"!

Well, Timothy was the leader-discipler of a group of Christians in this great city of

> art,
> religion,
> magic, and
> the occult.

Timothy lived there, felt its influence, sought to live out the gospel in its environment. He couldn't escape Ephesus to be a Christian. He had to live his life in the city just the way it was.

We share that with him. We are not free of our society. We live our Christian lives within our culture. It doesn't help to wish for another time or place or simpler lifestyle.

We live where we live and our lives are influenced by our surroundings.

Timothy had another context. His spiritual heritage is one with which many of us can identify—HE WAS A THIRD-GENERATION CHRISTIAN. His grandmother Lois and his mother, Eunice, passed the faith on to him. Paul makes it clear: Timothy had his own faith but he didn't originate it; he was brought up in it, as many of us have been.

My own granddad, now in heaven, was known as Uncle Bud Robinson. He was converted out of the rough; he began a Christian family heritage which I share. I'M A THIRD-GENERATION CHRISTIAN. Some of you are first, or second; most of you are third or fourth or fifth.

I'm thinking it was not an unmixed blessing for Timothy to have the kind of spiritual background he had. Nothing is said of his grandfather, and we know only that his father was a Greek. Did Timothy grow up in a home with strong religious women and weak, irreligious men? *Maybe that's one reason he had stomach trouble* (1 Timothy 5:23).

There are people upon whom **we** are dependent for our faith. We have gratitude toward them and for them. But sometimes there is resentment, too. We are struggling to find our own identity and grow in our own faith. Sometimes those who share the faith with us want to control our choices and structure our responses, pressuring us to conform.

I think Timothy experienced that kind of pressure. He had his Ephesian cultural environment, his own struggle to be his own person and find and live out his own faith. IF HE WAS LIKE THE REST OF US, THE FAITH IN HIM WAS NOT UNMIXED. Along with strong faith were some
> doubts and
>> fears and
>>> questions and
>>>> gropings and
>>>>> insecurities.

At the same time, he was trying to be a man of God and the discipler he ought to be. *I think I understand this man, don't you!*

Timothy had another context. Loved ones had passed on the faith to him but it was passed on in the context of a tradition and a doctrine. We understand that too, don't we? Our faith is received and lived out in the context of the traditions and doctrines of our church. That's good because God knows we don't need to live out our faith simply on the basis of our own
> personal whims
>> fancies
>>> moods
>>>> interests and
>>>>> influences.

WE REALLY DO NEED EACH OTHER AND WE REALLY DO NEED THE BODY OF BELIEVERS, THE CHURCH!

But having the church is not without its problems for us. We either go with the authoritative word of the church or rebel against tradition and whatever is vogue. All of us, like Timothy, have the task of working out our own salvation in relation to those who passed it on to us, and the church heritage through which it came to us, and the doctrinal position in which it was expressed. It is a necessary but not an easy task!

And then for Timothy there was Paul. How would you like to have St. Paul as

    your spiritual father

        your discipler

            your mentor and

                your district superintendent

                    all at the same time?

It would be wonderful and it would also be

                overwhelming

           frustrating and sometimes

        downright impossible!

Timothy wanted Paul's approval, needed his guidance, and desired very much to be like him, but he wasn't. *I guess that's why he needed something for his stomach's sake. Folks in the church that are my age take Pepto Bismol!*

Well, all this is simply to say that we are not without our contexts and it is necessary for us to recognize, accept, and relate to them; both the good and the bad in them.

Some of you are in the midst of great tension and stress in relation to those who have passed on to you the precious faith which is yours.

Some of you are having great problems with your own faith—trying to find out who you are and what you believe.

Many of you are in the process of finding your own stance or posture toward the church. You are asking the same inevitable questions:

What is my place in the church?

What are my feelings and responses to its

traditions

doctrines

rules

cultural and behavioral expectations?

How does all this relate to my own life and faith and the call of God

upon my life?

These are not easy questions and I have to say to you that I think some of you HAVE COPPED OUT ON THEM, AND TAKEN THE WAY OF EITHER CHANGE OR CONFORMITY WITHOUT REAL HEART ATTACHMENT!

I even think some of you have learned formulas and absorbed the lingo and imitated the behavior till you can turn them on and off at your own convenience. *Well, like Timothy, we do have our contexts, don't we?*

It is precisely at this point that we need to hear the word of the Lord in this passage of scripture. This is the word I am hearing:

the real problem is not the culture

the real problem is not with those who passed on the faith to us

the real problem is not with the church and its

tradition or

doctrine or

subculture or

whatever.

THE REAL PROBLEM IS FEAR! IT IS TIMIDITY! I must tell
you that I really believe that! I believe it for myself and for you.

Timothy's way of coping with the stresses of his context was to

withdraw,

pull in,

defend,

protect,

and so, escape the pressures of facing the real and staggering issues
of his time. We can do that, too. We can stand back and not get
involved and keep free and clear. There are many ways to back away.
That's my testimony!

I think I believe that it is not an easy thing to be a Christian in
today's world. It may be easy to be "born again." It is not easy
to answer the question: What does it mean to be a Christian? A
Disciple?

I know that it is not an easy thing for a college to be Christian. It
is not an easy thing for a church to be God's church, the body of
Christ, and to really become God's people. It is no simple thing for a
group of young people in a local church to find God's pattern for life
and then really seek to follow it.

I guess I'm really talking for myself. This passage of Scripture probes
me too deeply for comfort. I am an escapist, an expert in withdrawal.
*I am president of our local Cowards Club. (We will have a meeting of all local
presidents as soon as it gets dark tonight.)*

The Lord has been saying to me that **we cannot escape our culture.** But that overwhelming cultural environment we fear is the **object** of the redeeming love of God and is the **arena** into which we are sent as agents of His reconciliation and instruments of His peace!

Nor can we ignore the churchly tradition of our spiritual heritage. These are not really our problems, folks. Our problem is OURSELVES, OUR FEAR, OUR TIMIDITY!

So let us hear the word of the Lord. God has given us a gift. We who are weak and inadequate, in the face of the overwhelming task, have been given a grace-gift. IT IS THE GIFT OF GOD'S OWN SPIRIT. There is no need for fear, for timidity, for escapism.

We have the precious grace-gift of the **Spirit of God**! Paul describes the Spirit we have been given as the Spirit of

> power and
> love and
> self-control.

Let's talk about them.

From the study of Second Timothy, I have discovered that when God gives us His Spirit of power, it is not a gift that lifts us above the problems and struggles and needs of our common life. Pay attention to this line: "Share . . . [in] . . . suffering for the gospel in the power of God" (2 Timothy 1:8).

Can we ever believe that the power of God is released even in our weakness? Is the power of God at work when a timid person tremblingly shares the witness of God's grace? The power of God is not something that relieves us from pain and struggle but rather

sustains us
> and works through us
>> at the point of weakness and inadequacy
>>> as we are caringly
>>>> involved with persons.

Would you believe that the power of God to redeem mankind is expressed in a cross where the Son of God dies exhausted and abandoned?

Did you know that New Testament people proclaimed that that great moment of ultimate weakness was a manifestation of the "power of God for salvation to everyone who has faith" (Romans 1:16)?!

So it is with us. The grace-gift of His Spirit of power enables us, human as we are, to hold steady, to face issues, and to take whatever suffering comes to us as we try to be true to the call of God on our lives.

The gift of His Spirit is the gift of love. Here, too, Paul's word to Timothy helps us with a definition. I know and so do you, in spite of sentimental verses, that love is NOT a special way of feeling. IT IS A SPECIAL WAY OF BEHAVING! It is a special way of thinking and acting.

Listen to this:

> May the Lord grant mercy to the household of Onesiphorus, for he often refreshed me; he was not ashamed of my chains, but when he arrived in Rome he searched for me eagerly and found me (2 Timothy 1:16).

There, folks, is a definition of love! That's the kind of love that God has for us in Jesus, who is not ashamed of our bondage but comes to us with redeeming, lifting grace to help and to save. IT IS THE KIND OF LOVE THAT HIS SPIRIT IMPARTS TO US! Love is not ashamed to go where the despised person is, not ashamed to get helpfully involved.

The gift of His Spirit is the gift of self-control. Now, I don't like that word, self-control, any more than you do. But it is a good word and it is God's gift for us. It is not the spirit of ecstasy but the spirit of self-discipline and controlled living.

In Paul's letter to Timothy, he urges him not to get involved in senseless and needless chatter, not to become involved in stupid religious arguments but to give heed to the truth, pay attention to the Word, and hang on to the doctrine. I hear Paul say to Timothy and to me and to us all: **LIVE A LIFE OF DISCIPLINE AND LEARNING, AND TAKE YOUR SHARE OF HARDSHIP AS A GOOD SOLDIER OF CHRIST.**

I'm well aware that our sensuous world is more interested in ecstasy than in **discipline**. That word, however, if we hear it, really hear it, is a good and healing word.

Let me talk about it from my own point of view. I am privileged to live among the young who love spiritual feelings and spiritual ecstasy. *How many songs do you know that tell of the feelings of loving Jesus and being loved by Him?*

Some of the young persons I know are free to feel, to be "led by the Spirit," to go anywhere and float free in the Lord. But I am not that free.

I am married
and have a family
and have bills to pay
and classes to meet
and a lawn to mow.

It really doesn't matter how I feel. I've got to get up tomorrow and go to work. If the Spirit of God cannot minister to me in the ordinary life that I live with its

> problems
>> hassles
>>> burdens
>>>> duties
>>>>> routines;

Then I guess I am a second-class citizen in the Kingdom, *and that doesn't bless me at all!*

Oh, there are times of joy. There are even times of ecstasy. But the grace-gift God has given us is the gift of His own Spirit;

the gift of enablement
>to become sufferingly involved;

the gift of a love
>that is not ashamed to identify with someone who is not *in*;

the gift of self-discipline
>that doesn't seek to escape duty and routine

>but goes ahead to pick up the load, do the work, carry on.

You know, that really helps me!

Here is the key exhortation of the passage: **Rekindle the gift!**
Rekindle the fires of the grace-gift. The word for "gift" is *charisma*.
I like that. It means I'VE got charisma. It means YOU'VE got

charisma. It is the charisma of God's own Spirit which we share as members of His Body.

I have been asking God to stir up in me His gift, to rekindle the charisma. I'm not sure how rekindling takes place or what it means to "stir up the gift." I think it means, at least for me, letting the Spirit **reshuffle my priorities** as I give new attention to His presence in my life. I think it means **being obedient to the insights** that come as I reflect and meditate in His presence in prayer. I think it means **bringing my life into closer harmony** with what God is wanting to do with me. I'm sure it means these things for us all.

The culture will not go away.

We still must live with those who have passed on the faith to us.

We still live in the context of our tradition.

We still face the hard question of what it means to be disciples. But we have a gift! What we need we already have! **It is the grace-gift of God's own Spirit that helps us overcome fear and release the spirit of power, love, and self-control.**

Bow your heads with me.

O Jesus, here we are in the contexts of our lives and the Word comes to us as it came to Timothy. Give us grace and strength to rekindle the charisma, the grace-gift, that we received from Thee and to fan into flame the holy fire of Thy presence in us. In Thy name. Amen.

2
Saved Is a Big Word
2 Timothy 1:8-12

What are your
    dreams and
        goals and
            ideals as a Christian?

If you really were
        "what God wanted you to be,"
      if you really were "filled with the Holy Spirit,"
    if you really were all that you think you ought to be,
what would you be like?

Do you know what I'm thinking? A lot of what we visualize is pure
fantasy.

I am learning from the Word of God that if I am all I ought to be
and filled with the Spirit like I ought to be, the life that I live will be
very normal. It will be on this earth, involved with real, live things.

I will face temptation and experience failure. I will know some suffering. *I didn't used to believe that but I do now.*

And I wonder if some of our self-projections and self-images are fantasy. The problem is that when we judge ourselves by fantasy, WE ALWAYS COME UP SHORT.

I think if we will really give attention to what is in Second Timothy, it will help us to keep our feet on the real world and help us where we actually live.

Look at this:

> [8] Do not be ashamed then of testifying to our Lord, nor of me his prisoner, but share in suffering for the gospel in the power of God, [9] who saved us and called us with a holy calling, not in virtue of our works but in virtue of his own purpose and the grace which he gave us in Christ Jesus ages ago, [10] and now has manifested through the appearing of our Savior Christ Jesus, who abolished death and brought life and immortality to light through the gospel. (2 Timothy 1:8-10).

Isn't that a remarkable passage? Paul is in the process of encouraging Timothy. As we know, he has his own

weaknesses

problems

discouragements

shame and

timidity.

Paul seeks to encourage Timothy by showing him the direct
relationship between what he is facing in his tasks at Ephesus and the
> sovereign
>> eternal
> gracious
> saving
purposes of God.

Paul shows Timothy the direct relationship between what he is
> doing
>> facing
>>> living and
>>>> experiencing at Ephesus
AND the
>>> sovereign
>> eternal
> gracious
> saving
purposes of God.

And Timothy needed that. I think we do too.

It interests me that Paul often takes that approach. For instance, in
First Corinthians 12 and 14, he is facing the problem of divisions
and fragmentation in the Body of Believers, caused by the proud
exercise of various gifts. And in the middle of it all he gives us First
Corinthians 13 and shares with us the selfless love that is expressed
in the life of Jesus. He goes from local church divisions to the love of
First Corinthians 13.

In Philippians, Paul is talking about the relationship that we should
have with each other in terms of humility and lowliness and self-

forgetfulness; and he lifts that right up to talk about the self-emptying of Christ

> [6] who, though he was in the form of God, did not count equality with God a thing to be grasped, [7] but emptied himself, taking the form of a servant, being born in the likeness of men. [8] And being found in human form he humbled himself and became obedient unto death, even death on a cross. (Philippians 2:6-8).

HE CAME DOWN TO WHERE WE ARE! That great passage speaks of the humiliation of Jesus in the Incarnation and is intimately tied to our selfish relationships with each other.

In Second Corinthians Paul is talking about offerings and he closes with that incomparable line: "Thanks be to God for his inexpressible gift!" (2 Corinthians 9:15). He is talking about what it does for us when we give, and he ties it intimately to God's giving in Jesus Christ.

And in Ephesians Paul is talking about relationships:
> fathers and children
> slaves and masters
> husbands and wives.

Suddenly he lifts us to the great purpose of God in Christ when he says:

> [25] Husbands, love your wives, as Christ loved the church and gave himself up for her, [26] that he might sanctify her, having cleansed her by the washing of water with the word, [27] that he might present the church to himself in splendor, without spot or wrinkle or any such thing, that she might be holy and without blemish. (Ephesians 5:25-27).

Do you see what he does? He moves from the
>   common
>   ordinary
>   issues of life to the
>   sovereign
>   gracious
purposes of God.

And I have been thinking about that. When I'm hassling with all the
fragmentation that I face in the Body of Believers with
>   all the varieties of gifts
>   all the status symbols and
>   ecclesiastical divisions and
>   pigeon holes,
I hardly ever think of First Corinthians 13!

When I am trying to be a Jesus-loving person in the midst of the
establishment, trying to keep my relationships with my peers, those
above me and under me, the way they ought to be, I hardly ever
think of the self-emptying of Jesus!

When I go to church and put in our check for tithes and offerings, I
hardly ever think about God giving Jesus!

And when I'm trying to be a decent husband, I hardly ever think
that my relationship with Mary Jo should be like that of Christ and
His church! BUT PAUL DID!

I have been thinking that
>   in our sufferings
>   in our struggles
>   in our encounters in daily life

we do not relate ourselves to the sufferings of Jesus.

>   We relate our victories to the power of the Holy Spirit.
>   We relate our successes to the joy of God.
>   When we are delivered from suffering, we thank God.

But when we are in the midst of suffering, we seldom think about the power of God or relate our suffering to the suffering of Jesus!

I wonder if it is a kind of false ego that makes that possible. We suffer alone and hardly ever relate our

> sufferings
>> hassles
>>> divisions
>>>> personal relationships

to what God is doing in Jesus!

Timothy was having the same problem, and Paul just lifted his vision and said some things that I'd like to emphasize: **"Timothy, take your share of suffering in the power of God who saved us!"**

He's not moving away from suffering; he's gathering it up into something bigger.

> He's relating it to the God who saved us
>> and called us with a holy calling.
> He is relating it to the revelation of the saving purposes
>> available to us in Jesus Christ.

Folks, did you know that **God is a saving God?**

Paul related the
> experiences
>> struggles

and sufferings
that Timothy had, to the
     sovereign
    eternal
   saving
  gracious
purposes of God!

He saved us and called us with a holy calling!

I wish there was a way to take the word "saved" and spread it out and make it bigger than we normally think of it. Behind the word "saved" is the big word "salvation," which I have come to believe is about the biggest word in God's book.

We talk about getting "saved and sanctified," and I believe in that. But it doesn't describe all that God is doing. ALL of God's purposes in our lives are saving purposes. And so, by the great saving intention of God in the world, we experience His grace, His saving grace.

Did you know the
  sovereign
    eternal
      Creator
       Father God
has a purpose in our world? That purpose is to save
       to heal
      to redeem
     to renew
    to unite
   to reconcile
to move into every area where sin has left

    estrangement
       hostility
          darkness and
            death
to move into every area with
            healing
            lift
            light
            joy?

GOD WANTS TO SAVE! HE IS A SAVING GOD!

I find my own life caught up in those saving purposes. In fact, all God's dealings with us are **saving** dealings. God's providences in my life and in yours are **saving** providences.

I think of all the influences that have played upon our lives where the saving presence of God has been at work. I think about
    His convicting work
        His forgiving grace in our lives
           how He leads us
               the cleansing work of the Holy Spirit
                   in sanctifying power.
I think about
              our life together in the Body of Believers
       the encounters
     and ministries
in fellowship and work.

God's intention is a saving intention!

Actually, I am one of the most saved men you ever saw:

I have been saved
and been saved
and been saved.
I don't know if you identify with that or not.

I have been born again
    and again
    and again
    and again.
I can remember the times and can tell you the places where the Lord came in and saved me by His graces!

I'll tell you something else: I am **being** saved and so are you!

And I see what is going on these days as a saving work of God. Now, saving in this sense means that God is
    cleansing
      strengthening
        teaching
          guiding
            rebuking
              chastising
                judging
              bringing to repentance
          new faith
        new life
      new insight
    new relationships
new understandings.
In all of this we are being **saved**. However, one of these days we will **be saved**. Thank God!

You know what I am going to say when I get to heaven?

I'm saved.

I have been saved.

I am being saved.

I will be saved.

Praise God!

I think a good response to the question, "Are you saved?" is: "Have been, are being, will be!" In other words, the answer is **YES! YES! YES!**

I think that is why I like the gospel song:

"Life now is sweet

and my joy is complete

for I'm saved, saved, saved!"

from *Saved, Saved!*

Words and Music by Jack P. Scholfield, 1911

Folks, the sovereign, eternal, Creator God has a saving intention in our world! I don't know where God is for you, but get Him out of heaven and get Him down in the world! He doesn't sit up there like some skinny Buddha with a long beard. He doesn't sit like Abraham Lincoln on a stone throne with space around Him. **GET HIM DOWN OUT OF HEAVEN AND INVOLVED SAVINGLY IN THE WORLD!**

Now don't pass over some of those other words in that passage—that God manifests, makes known, His saving purposes in His world by the appearing of Jesus Christ.

The **appearing**. What does that mean? It means the visible manifestation of the eternal God. **God has come to us in Jesus.**

We believe that the
>> sovereign
> eternal
Creator
Father God

has **Himself** entered into the arena of human life in Jesus Christ our Lord!

We believe that eternity has come in time
> the Father has come in the Son
>> and light has come into our darkness
>>> and life has come into our death

in the appearing of our Lord and Savior, Jesus Christ. **That is Incarnation!**

Here is what Christians believe the most and best of all: God is the kind of person that if He ever had a son, He'd be just like Jesus! *I'm so old I can make that childish statement and not even be embarrassed!* God is the kind of person that if He would ever decide to come into our world to help us, He'd send someone like Jesus! That is, in fact, what we believe!

DID YOU KNOW THAT ALL OUR EGGS ARE IN THIS BASKET AND WE ARE OUT ON A LIMB?!

What we are saying is that God encounters the evil of the world with His saving purposes by himself entering into the arena of our struggle, taking onto himself the meaning of
> evil
> sin
> sorrow
> estrangement

and trying to help.

God's way of dealing with evil in our world is by His own personal, loving, suffering involvement with it, even unto death! And so, He abolished death by taking it into himself, going all the way to experience what it means.

As it says in the Apostles' Creed about our Lord Jesus Christ:
Conceived by the Holy Spirit,
born of the Virgin Mary,
suffered under Pontius Pilate,
was crucified, dead, and buried;
descended into Hades.

He encountered the evil of the world by entering into it ultimately, to the death. Then the power of God reversed the course of nature and brought Jesus back from the dead and enthroned Him at His right hand in power and glory. **He brought life and immortality to light through the gospel!**

So, Timothy, and all the rest of us timid folk, need to see that in and through all that is happening, God is expressing His saving purposes entering lovingly, and sufferingly, into the arena of our struggles **AND GOING ALL THE WAY WITH US!**

Now this God who saves us has also called us with a holy calling. We are a **saved** people. We are a **called** people.

The God who saves by suffering care has called us into a fellowship involving suffering love with Him.
Ours is a holy calling
from the holy God
to be a holy people
in fulfillment of His holy purposes.

We find our own fulfillment as we participate in the saving purposes of God!

Aren't you glad that the salvation and calling we share are not according to our own work but according to His own purpose and grace revealed in Jesus? It is a great thing to know that our salvation doesn't rest on our own efforts or struggles, that it doesn't depend on the level of our psychic energy. **We are not the victims of our moods or our dispositions!**

I remember my old granddad saying that one time, shortly after he was converted, he woke up one morning with a dark brown taste in his mouth. He said, "I've slept off my religion!" *I understand that feeling, don't you?* But he hadn't slept it off! It was too great, too secure a religion to lose that way.

> God is the Do-er
>> and we are the do-ees.
> God is the Initiator
>> and we are the responders.
So our faith does not rest on what we can do but on the
> sovereign
>> eternal
>>> purposes of God
>>>> manifested in Jesus Christ
>>>>> displayed ultimately on the Cross
>>>>>> immortalized in the power
>>>>>>> of the Resurrection.

I can feel the joy of Paul when he declares, "For this gospel I was appointed a preacher and apostle and teacher, and therefore I suffer as I do" (2 Timothy 1:11-12a).

What is that last line doing there?! It doesn't go with the rest of the paragraph. Our last line would be: "and therefore,

> I proclaim as I do,
>
> and succeed as I do,
>
> and get all my prayers answered!"

And once I missed a plane but God was in it because it crashed and I was spared and besides, it was full of Baptists! Thank God I was saved from suffering!

NO! It doesn't end that way!

For this gospel we too are appointed

> proclaimers
>
> and witnesses
>
> and disciplers
>
> **and therefore, suffer as we do!**

But suffering isn't the final word either. "But I am not ashamed, for I know whom I have believed, and I am sure that he is able to guard until that Day what has been entrusted to me" (2 Timothy 1:12b).

We know what the gospel is and what the saving purposes of God are. Isn't it a marvelous privilege to know the God of the saving gospel? We can enter into personal fellowship with God. We can know the gospel—but more, we can know the personal God of the gospel! He is the God who is able to keep what He has deposited with us safe and secure!

What has He given to you?

Forgiveness?

Cleansing?

Your life?

Your meaning

and place

and ministry?

He will guard them safe!

I am thinking about His saving grace, the good things He has given, the gifts of

family

love

place

ministry

sense of meaning

worth and hope.

All these and 10,000 besides! **He is able to keep and guard them until the final day!**

There is another way to look at it. He is able to guard what we have given to Him. What have you given Him? What are you giving Him now?

Your sins?

Guilts and failures?

Your hopes and dreams?

Yourself?

He will guard them safely! It is His promise forever!

Well, it is a great gospel and He is a great God. AND WE LIVE IN A GREAT TENSION. On the one hand is

> our world
>> our humanness
>>> our weakness
>>>> and suffering.

On the other hand is the

>>> gracious
>> saving
> purpose and

power of God.

They both are real, and this passage in Second Timothy is telling me, and telling us all, to **open up our worlds to Him to give to Him who we are and what we do.**

Don't separate your failures from Him.

Don't separate your sufferings from Him.

Don't separate your weaknesses from the power of the gospel!

Our human lives are related to His gracious purposes and **He will never let us down. Praise God!**

3
Remember Jesus
2 Timothy 2:8-13

I haven't been able to quit thinking about a beautiful heavy phrase in Second Timothy. "Remember Jesus Christ, risen from the dead, descended from David, as preached in my gospel" (2 Timothy 2:8).

As I have been thinking about that line and letting it speak in my own heart, two or three things have emerged. One is this: At the heart of our gospel, at the center of our religion, is a **Person**. The center of Christianity

is not a doctrine

is not an idea

is not a truth

is not **the** Truth

is not a concept

is not a world view

is not an attitude

is not a stance or

a way of looking at things.

The center of our religion is a **Person**.

Now, when I say that it doesn't sound so profound, but I am here to tell you it has been a changing factor in my life and is at the heart of the revolution that is continuing inside me as I am trying to learn what it means to be a disciple.

THE HEART OF OUR RELIGION IS NOT SOMETHING BUT SOMEONE.

Eric Frost said, "Real Christian experience comes from the meeting of our souls with Christ, not just a brief encounter but the coming alive of a lasting relationship, personal and unique." *Isn't that good?*

You know at the center of
>   Buddhism
>   Confucianism
>   Hinduism
>   Unity
>   Science of Mind
>   Christian Science
>   Hare Krishna—
is an idea
>   a truth
>   a worldview
>   an understanding
>   or a point of view.
Do you want to think about that for a minute?

>   The heart of Buddhism
>   is a way of looking at the universe.
>   The heart of Hinduism

is the way that relates to ultimate reality.

The heart of Christian Science, Unity, Science of Mind,

is a stance or posture or way of looking at things.

The understanding of what is true or what is real becomes the focal point from which life, behavior and values emerge.

But the heart of the Christian faith is not a world view or way of looking at things or an understanding of reality. **THE HEART OF CHRISTIAN FAITH IS A PERSON.**

That's why I think that doctrine in evangelical circles is always a matter of hassle and is never finally, precisely expressed. That's good and bad. We suffer from doctrinal imprecision. *Now, I don't know what that phrase means exactly, but I just like the way it sounds!*

For example, we go from east to west from north to south and isn't it wonderful, that we have one precise, clear definition of sanctification? *Isn't that a blessing? Whatever else you can say about us we all believe it the same way. All Nazarenes know exactly and precisely what it is and how we get it!*

But that's really all right because the ultimate reality is not the ability to express doctrine with precision. Think about it this way: when we bring people to Christ we do not indoctrinate, we **introduce**.

I suppose we could get records and books and go two by two and indoctrinate the world. However, for better or for worse, *and I think for better*, we don't go that route.

THE CENTER OF OUR GOSPEL IS NOT SOMETHING; IT IS SOMEONE.

And Protestants are either wise enough, or stupid enough, to believe that if we will introduce persons to Him who is the center, His Spirit who is the Spirit of Truth, will be the one to guide them into Truth.

The older I get the more willing I am, I think, to trust the teaching ministry of the Holy Spirit. If we get close to Jesus, and stay close to Jesus, and keep open and sensitive to His teaching Spirit, we won't go all that far into left field.

> Where we rest
>> where we live
>>> who we are
>>>> what we are
>>> our hopes
>> and dreams
> and values
>> our fight for authenticity
>>> and integrity
>>>> does not rest on doctrine.

It rests on a **Person**.

And all of our relationships with God and all of our relationships with Jesus are **personal**.

When we get saved, we don't get something, we enter into a relationship with **Someone**. And when the tears are dried and the emotions have subsided, what is left over is a relationship. And when all our doctrinal words are finished, when we're sanctified, what we end up with is a quality relationship with a **Person**.

At the heart of our gospel is a Person, Jesus Christ!

Paul tells Timothy to remember Jesus Christ. That's an interesting word, isn't it? I have been thinking about the word "remember." When we say, remember, we have in mind the recall of something or someone. *I will never forget what's-his-face. I remember his name as well as mine. Oh, yes, I remember that.* Well, that's the way we use it, normally.

Let me use this illustration to explain how the wonderful word, remember, is used in Scripture. I have a mental image of a mother with a five-year-old getting ready to go into the supermarket. Before they go into this wonderland, I see the mother say to the child who is listening intently, "Do you remember what I said to you?" And the proper response is not, "Yeah, I remember what you said." The proper response is, "OK, I will stay close to you. I will obey."

FOLKS, WE ARE TO *REMEMBER* JESUS CHRIST!

That doesn't mean we are to remember that such a Person lived. The word carries with it a sense of observance. What is to be remembered in the Bible is not simply brought to mind, it is

> brought to heart and
> made present in the life and
> calls for response.

I'm sure you have sung that great old spiritual, *that I can do without,* "Do Lord, Oh, Do Lord." *You know when we get to heaven, I'm going to go somewhere where nobody sings, "Do Lord"!* However, in it is a very good word: "Do **remember** me." Does that mean, "Lord, just remember me"?

"Oh, yes, son, I remember you." No. It means, "Keep me in mind, Lord, observe me, relate to me, hold me in Your thoughts and in Your heart."

When God said, "Remember the sabbath day to keep it holy," how do we remember? "Oh, I remember, it's Sunday. How come I forgot that last week?" That doesn't quite fulfill the command, does it? How do we remember the Sabbath Day? We observe it to keep it holy, that's how it is remembered.

God said, "I will cause my name to be remembered." "Oh, I remember what Your name is, God." *Jehovah or Yahweh, if you've been to seminary.*

David prayed, "Remember not the sins of my youth nor my transgressions."

When our children began to get a little older and would go out on their own, Mary Jo would often say to our son, Rob, "Remember who you are!" and he'd go out the door saying, "Oh, yes, my name's Rob."

I will never forget the time we went to a Junior-Senior Banquet at the College and Mary Jo was dressed in a beautiful gown and I was in a tux. We started out the door, and Rob said, "Mom, remember who you are!" We knew what he had in mind.

"Jesus, remember me when you come into your kingdom" (Luke 23:42), the thief on the cross prayed.

What does it mean to remember Jesus? I am not sure I really know. What does it mean to forget Him? To forget Jesus certainly doesn't mean that we forget there was a Jesus-Person who lived. To forget Him would be to ignore

    reject

    act as though He were not present.

I have come to believe that the exhortation for us to remember Jesus
is really helpful. We don't forget Him on purpose but so often we just
>> neglect
>> ignore
>> or are just preoccupied.

But if we are remembering Jesus
>> we are holding Him in our attention
>>> we are holding Him precious in our hearts
>>>> reverent in our thoughts
>>> hallowing His name
>> observing Him.

I am thinking that Jesus himself said, "Do this in remembrance of
me" (Luke 22:19). And when we break the bread and drink the cup,
we are holding Him present and precious so that His very presence is
brought into our real presence and we worship as we **remember**.

There are a couple of things about remembering Jesus that Paul
indicates in the passage. One is this: That He "descended from
David" (2:8). Jesus is a real, live Person
>>>> with a family tree
>>>>> with brothers and sisters
>>>>>> and uncles and aunts
>>>>> and cousins and nephews
>>>> and grandfolks.

He did not come into our world out of nowhere. He entered into it
totally. He came from a tribe of people with a family history and a
family tree. He had a genealogy. Jesus descended from David. He
participates in what it means to be a part of the human family.

I say that to you, in spite of the fact that we all know it, because it took me nearly 50 years to believe, *and I do believe from the depths of my heart.* You see, I have believed all my life that Jesus is truly divine but the understanding that Jesus is truly human has been hard to come by for me.

I want to tell you what I believe utterly and deeply: that from the human point of view, **Jesus is as human as we are**, and from the divine point of view, **Jesus is just as divine as His Father.** All we can finally say by way of explanation is that we cannot let go of either His **humanity** or His **divinity**.

We have a tendency to believe that the fundamental reality is the divinity of Jesus, that His humanity is a temporary relationship, a shallow encounter. But I believe that when our Lord Jesus left the splendors of His Father and entered into the arena of our human struggle and into the flow of our human history, **He came all the way**.

He knows what it means to be human.

He knows utterly what it is to participate in the human situation
    with its alienation
    estrangement
    limitations of knowledge
    and understanding.
He knows about the temptations
    hassles and
    stress of living.
HE KNOWS WHAT IT MEANS TO BE HUMAN! Hallelujah!

I believe when our Lord went back to His Father, somewhere along the way He left His physical body but He did not release His humanity. And Jesus is our brother, now. He is just as human now as He ever was when He walked the dusty trails of Palestine. He entered utterly into our humanity and I know that there is no gap between Jesus and God. But let me tell you something else, folks, **there is no gap between Jesus and me!**

I look up to Him, but I also look straight across at Him
> eyeball to eyeball
> life to life
> bone to bone
> person to Person.

And the Jesus we **remember** is utterly human like we are.

> For we have not a high priest who is unable to sympathize with our weaknesses, but one who in every respect has been tempted as we are, yet without sinning (Hebrews 4:15).

I believe that. I really do!

That does not mean, of course, that Jesus experienced all the temptations of a single male or female in the 20th century. But He did experience totally what it means to be human. Remember, Jesus Christ descended from David. That's our family too, the human family.

Paul tells us, as he told Timothy, that this human Jesus is risen from the dead. Amen! **Jesus is risen from the dead!** Do you know that Jesus has experienced death? That is the ultimate of human experience and He has shared totally in what it means.

Then the Father raised Him from the dead and exalted Him at His right hand. And the glory of the Christian gospel is this:

God comes to us in Jesus
all the way to where we are
identifying totally with us
at the point of our humanity.
But He is able by the power of His resurrection to bring into our lives
a strength and
a power and
a dynamic greater than our own. **Hallelujah!**

You know, if Jesus is only related to God and partially related to us there is still space between us. If Jesus is totally related to us but only partially related to God then there is space between us and God. But the glory of the gospel is that God himself comes all the way to where we are so **there isn't any space between us and God!**

As H. Orton Wiley said a long time ago, "With one arm Jesus reaches into the loving heart of the Father and with the other he reaches into the broken heart of a lost humanity, and in himself he brings the two together."

Remember Jesus Christ! This person, with whom we may have intimate personal fellowship through His Spirit, is human as we are but is risen from the dead! So, the secret and the power of the Christian believer is that **by our side is One who truly walks with us and is able to bring into our life a power and a glory greater than our own!**

Well then, Paul says, "The saying is sure: if we have died with him, we shall also live with him" (2 Timothy 2:11). Amen!

The death He died is more than something out there done for us, it is something in which we participate. There **is** a kind of life without death to self, but it isn't resurrection life.

Resurrection life for us is on the far side of death! "If we have died with him, we shall also live with him. If we endure, we shall also reign with him" (2 Timothy 2:11-12a). *Here's a hard line*, "If we deny him, he also will deny us" (2 Timothy 2:12b).

You know, that is virtually a quote from what Jesus said to the disciples in His charge to the Twelve:

> [32] So every one who acknowledges me before men, I also will acknowledge before my Father who is in heaven; [33] but whoever denies me before men, I also will deny before my Father who is in heaven (Matthew 10:32-33).

I have been trying to understand what that means. In Matthew 10 Jesus was talking to His disciples. It was not really a salvation issue but a ministering issue. And Paul is talking not to sinners but to Timothy.

What we have here is probably part of an early Christian hymn. There is a stern warning, isn't there? But listen to the bottom line: "If we are faithless, he remains faithful—for he cannot deny himself" (2 Timothy 2:13).

As I have looked at that hymn, I have noticed this: the rhythm of it is broken and the logic is broken: "If we have died with him, we shall also live with him…If we endure [with him] we shall also reign with him" (2 Timothy 2:11-12). *So far so good. I understand that.* "If we deny him, he also will deny us; if we are faithless, he remains faithful" (2 Timothy 2:12-13).

The love of God and the faithfulness of God break into the human logic and the cycle of inevitability because the faithful God is faithful **in spite of our unfaithfulness!** Isn't it a wonderful thing to know that our believing it doesn't make it true, and our denying it doesn't make it untrue? *Think about that!*

The ultimate base of who we are and what we are is the faithfulness of God, for He cannot deny himself! That means a lot to me in the flow of my own life
in its ups and downs
in the hard times
in the good times
in the adolescent times
in the mature times
in the times when I am dumb
and stupid
and childish
and petty
and the times when I think I am wise and wonderful.

In the midst of all that He remains faithful. He who has revealed himself in the human, risen Jesus, remains faithful. **GOD IS FAITHFUL!** Praise His name!

4
Words, Handle with Care

2 Timothy 2:14-19

I heard these words in a prayer: "The Word of God is like a letter written to us with our name on it." I have found that to be true in my own life as I have been working through Second Timothy. Especially as I read Second Timothy 2:14-19:

> [14] Remind them of this, and charge them before the Lord to avoid disputing about words, which does no good, but only ruins the hearers. [15] Do your best to present yourself to God as one approved, a workman who has no need to be ashamed, rightly handling the word of truth. [16] Avoid such godless chatter, for it will lead people into more and more ungodliness, [17] and their talk will eat its way like gangrene. Among them are Hymenaeus and Philetus, [18] who have swerved from the truth by holding that the resurrection is past already. They are upsetting the faith of some. [19] But God's firm foundation stands, bearing

this seal: "The Lord knows those who are his," and, "Let every one who names the name of the Lord depart from iniquity."

I have been surprised at the strange combination of ideas in this paragraph.

First: "Avoid disputing about words."

Then: "Do your best to present yourself to God as one approved."

Next: "Avoid such godless chatter."

Then: Follow the illustration of the two in the church who "swerved from the truth."

Last: The concluding verse reveals the seal or sign of "God's firm foundation."

I want to share with you the way these ideas are coming together in my mind and heart and how they are affecting my life. I speak clearly to people like you and me who are **word** people. We are not too good on doing, but we are really good with words. *Aren't we?*

Now, there are some words I would die for. Words like

God

Jesus

Holy Spirit

love

repentance

faith

joy

service

giving

"Thou art the Christ"

"My Lord and my God."

These words are the words that are everything to us. But you know, the words give us trouble too, don't they? And when Paul said to Timothy, don't get involved in useless, trivial arguments about words and don't get involved in disputes and religious debates because they don't do any good, he was saying something that we need to hear, *wasn't he?*

You know, we have a tendency to dispute about words, ideas and doctrines. And I have discovered that so often
>the words that we share
>the discussions
>the religious dialogues we get into
>have a tremendous amount of **ego involvement**.

I'm thinking how young preachers go off to school
>and major in religion
>>and read half a book
>>>and learn 14 new terms
>>>>and it just changes their lives.

They take the Sword of the Spirit
>>>and smite the foe right and left
>>bandying about words
>throwing around ideas
hassling about doctrine and concepts.

How much ego involvement is there in this? We are just about the best talkers that the Lord has in His great kingdom! There is something about our fellowship and the way we function that affirms the one who can use words.

I remember a long time ago when Susan was about two, I realized she must have been born talking. We were pastoring a church, and one Wednesday night when the people were sharing, she stood up on the seat and said, "I do love the Lord." Well, you know how the dear saints felt: "Oh, isn't that sweet." So, they were all warmed and blessed and Susan, of course, received all those warm fuzzies. Would you like to guess what she did the next Wednesday night? She stood up one more time, spoke louder, with gestures. *Do we understand each other?*

Well, when she grew up and got in a traveling singing group and went around with bright lights and a microphone, she had a problem because she was one of those kids who got saved when she was six. With bright lights and a microphone, her great story about what the Lord did for her at six left a little to be desired. She couldn't talk about a life full of sin and darkness and misery, only a life transformed at six.

I remember she came home one time really troubled because she realized she didn't have a testimony worth hearing. We talked quite a bit about it. *Do you understand how she felt?*

Well, we are word people. Don't think words are not important because they are. We live and die by them, and there are some we live and die **for**. *I must say that the ones that I would die for are getting fewer and fewer!*

Words are important but religious argumentation can be so destructive. The Lord has been talking to me about this. I have observed how much hurt has come about in religious arguments. I know families who are split over doctrine when fundamentally, there is about a quarter of an inch difference in both positions.

Anxiety

    animosity

        separation

> alienation and
> > hostility
emerge out of doctrinal and religious arguments!

I am hearing a new thing from Second Timothy: our religious discussions and debates, our throwing around all kinds of words may not be much of a blessing to those around us.

Someone put this on a 3 x 5 card and laid it on my desk:
> Jesus said, "Who do you say that I am?"
> And they said, "You are the eschatological manifestation of the ground of being; you are the *kerygma* magnified in conflict and decision in the humanizing process."
> And Jesus said: "What?"

Words, words, words. We love them, collect them, use them, but we may not know what they really mean. When we hear a new word, we think we have to go back and lay it on everybody. Some of the new thoughts and ideas that are radically life-transforming to you may not be an immediate blessing to those who haven't shared the same insights. Can we realize that in disputing about words, in communicating ideas, there is a tremendous amount of **ego** involved?

Did you ever think about how much useless religious talk goes on at cocktail parties, saloons, bars, even in places like Sunday School classes? When you gather up the strange things that people say about God, the trivial arguments people have that God has to listen to, I've wondered if God doesn't get tired of all the ridiculous things that are said about Him. I've wondered where God goes to escape? *You know something? He doesn't have any place to go!*

> He is God and He listens
> and listens

and listens
> while we pour forth all our ego-filled
> unwisdomed stupidities
> trying to right the wrongs of the world
> and get everybody straightened out
> and proclaim the truth.

I hear the word for me. I hear the call of God. "Do your best to present yourself to God as one approved" (2 Timothy 2:15).

So much of our talk with each other, so much of our dialogue is really not dialogue, it is traded monologue. Have you ever had the feeling when talking with people that they weren't really listening; they were waiting for you to shut up so that they could say what they wanted to say? No mutual quest for the truth but an ego-filled desire to show what we know, to lay the truth on others.

And then I hear the call of the Word of God, and I begin to see the paragraph come together. Paul says: "Timothy, don't be involved in all this kind of stuff, but present yourself as one approved of God." The final issue is not our words, words, words. The final issue is **The Word**: "Do your best to present yourself to God as one approved, a workman who has no need to be ashamed, rightly handling the word of truth." (2 Timothy 2:15).

How do you rightly handle the word of truth or the perspective or metaphor carried in the original language? How do you hold a straight course, cut a straight line through the word of truth?

The only thing I know for sure is this:
> when I am letting the Word speak to me
>> and I am trying to understand it
> without needless debate or argumentation

> nor for ego fulfillment
> or to show anybody how much I know
> or to lay it on somebody else
> but when I am being truly open to God
> and open to the Word
> it's marvelous how it does speak.

Isn't that a wonderful thing?

I have discovered when I am working through a passage to have something to say, that is one thing. But when, by the grace of God, I am enabled by His Spirit to lay all of that down and say, "Lord, what do You have to say to me?" That is quite another thing!

To change the point of reference from those around me to God himself makes the Word come alive to speak in ways that make a difference in my life! So that's my call and that's your call—to do your best to present yourself to God, "as one approved, a workman who has no need to be ashamed, rightly handling the word of truth."

Then Paul goes on to talk about Hymenaeus and Philetus who were passing around bad doctrine. But you know, Paul said you don't have to get involved in that either, because God's foundation is sure.

Let me share with you a new thing to me. In the world where I live, and I'm sure it's the same in the world where you live, there are some bad doctrines going around. I sometimes don't know what to think about all the weird ideas and doctrines floating around these days.

There is so much about witchcraft, witches and warlocks. We hear of
> Satan worship
> Hare Krishna
> Moonies.

Folks, there are weird doctrine and cults floating around all over the place!

I'm not going to get off on a tangent here, but I think that in our quest for

    upward mobility

        security

            individuality

                a comfortable lifestyle

we have subtly shifted from those great values in the Spirit that give life meaning, and are in danger of being sucked into the vacuum of the weird ideas our society has created.

I've got to say that at my ripe old age, I have a different attitude toward the desperate people who go into Transcendental Meditation, Oriental religion, communes, astrology. *Can you believe how many people are into astrology? It's ridiculous and destructive!*

I have changed from an attitude of judgment to an attitude of loving care and concern. However, when you think about all that is happening these days—the drug scene, the liquor scene—it seems to be a very poor time in history for sophisticated, Nazarene kids to begin experimenting with smoking or learning to drink a little wine, especially at the very time when the awesome destructiveness of all these things is emerging in stupendous proportions.

I think about these things and ask, "What is my place in all of this?" I have come to believe that underneath all of the movement into this, and into that, and into other things is a hunger for

    spiritual life

    spiritual relationships

    meaning and

    worth.

Maybe it is not a time for harsh judgment. But it is the time for the right kind of sharing.

You see, I don't have to refute all the errors going around. *Praise God! Isn't that wonderful? That, folks, is a great relief!*

I don't have to settle all the doctrinal issues and differences among us. I know there are errors in the great Body of Believers, and some of them eat their way like gangrene and are destructive. But the call of God to me is not to

> throw around my concepts
> defend my ego
> lay on everybody my thoughts
> > and ideas
> > and newly learned big words.

I don't have to do that. I don't have to refute all the errors. Hallelujah!

I hear the word of the Lord to Timothy telling me I don't have to worry about

> the differences we have in our fellowship
> > the differences of point of view
> of our understanding of the Holy Spirit's work;
> > what the Spirit does when He comes, or
> what is important in His activity.

I don't have to worry about them because God knows those who are His! Amen!

There are people like Hymenaeus and Philetus. There are errors around that are destructive but God knows those who are His and it's all right. Amen.

The foundation of God stands sure, and God really knows those who are His. He is in intimate fellowship with them. Hallelujah!

That releases me from the spirit of judgment and I don't have to decide
>who is in
>>and who is out
>who is right
>>and who is wrong.
God knows those who are His and I may rest in that.

The other thing I hear is the call of God on me in the midst of the words and diversities of
>thoughts
>ideas
>doctrines and
>teachings
to **live a holy life**. "Let every one who names the name of the Lord, depart from iniquity" (2 Timothy 2:19). That's His calling to me!

And as I take my place in the world, wherever God's providences place me, I can live in confidence because it rests finally on God's knowledge. I can respond to His call to live a holy life. I can keep working to hold a straight course in the Word of Truth. Praise God!

So that's where I am. That's what the paragraph has been saying to me. It isn't that there aren't doctrines to be refuted. It isn't that we do not need doctrinal precision. We do!

But our temptation is to get our egos involved and that becomes destructive! Here is what I am hearing: **God knows who is who and what is what.**

My call is **to live a holy life, and to hold a straight course in the words of Truth.** And I believe profoundly that in this context God can use me to be a

> healing
>
> lifting
>
> reconciling agent in His world.

Would you bow your heads a minute?

O Jesus, we are together and we're concerned about words. With so many of them around that communicate

> ideas
>
> doctrines
>
> thoughts and
>
> teachings

we sometimes wonder

> who we are
>
> what we are to say
>
> and what is the truth?

We are grateful that Thou art the Truth and we hear the word of the Lord, that Thou knowest who art thine. We rest in that today and don't have to live our lives in judgment. We don't have to flail about, tell everybody what we know, get the whole world straightened out **because Thou knowest who art Thine.**

And we hear again the call to live a holy life, to be obedient to the call of God who would bring us to himself and send us lovingly into His world.

Keep us close to Thy world, holding a straight course in it to show ourselves approved unto Thee. Then, Father, use us where we need to be used and we will be grateful. In Thy name we pray, Amen.

5
Biography Is Not Enough
2 Timothy 3:1-17

Let's go back and picture Timothy, pastor and bishop of Ephesus.
Paul says to him, and the Holy Spirit through Paul says to us: "In the
last days there will come times of stress" (2 Timothy 3:1).

As I have understood the passage to this point in my journey,
Timothy would have a particular kind of stress because he would be
in a society that was distinctly religious. But he would be surrounded
by "religious persons" who were

> lovers of pleasure
> lovers of self
> abusive
> willful
> treacherous
> lovers of money
> lovers of pleasure more than lovers of God.

Just take a look at that package. Men will be

>lovers of pleasure
>lovers of money
>egotistical
>proud
>boastful.

It is fascinating to me as I read the passage that it seems he is talking about pleasure without restraint. And when you have

>pleasure
>egotism
>pride
>boastfulness
>self-will
>love of money, it ends up in
>>abuse
>>destruction
>>sadism
>>cruelty
>>and masochism.

That's strange, isn't it?

As I was reading through the passage it dawned on me that the people of whom Paul speaks have "a form of religion." So we are **not** talking about the irreligious.

I can handle irreligious people being sensual, materialistic, pornographic, but when that moves inside the church, that causes **stress!**

I can handle Hugh Hefner and the *Playboy* philosophy because he is a child of the world, but when the editor of *Hustler* is supposedly "born again" without any life changes that causes **stress!** And I think that kind of thing caused stress for Timothy too.

It was a brand-new thing to me as I was working through the passage to see that all of this awesome description of

self-centeredness

ego

pride

sensualism

cruelty

heartlessness

was within the circle of **religion**, and that's what causes **distress!**

So here's Timothy, third-generation, trying to do his thing in Ephesus but inside the circle of religion are all these **stressful** features.

But, thank God, on the other side there is Paul, who represents the living out of the Spirit of Christ. He says there will be religious men who are like the world. But he also says you have observed

my teaching

my conduct

my faith

my patience

my steadfastness

my suffering

my enduring.

So on one hand we have those within the circle of religion whose lives in no way reflect the gospel and example of Christ. But on the other hand, we have the godly, holy persons represented by Paul who reflect Christ among us.

Then there is a line that fascinates me: "As for you, continue in what you have learned" (2 Timothy 3:14). And here is what I am seeing; I hope you can see it too. On the one hand you have

>the sensual
>>the proud
>>>the materialistic
>>>>the pornographic
>>>>>the cruel
>>>>>>the self-centered.

On the other hand, we have the beautiful people of God who reflect in life and behavior the ministry of Jesus Christ.

Now I come down to that line of Paul's that says, "As for you." Did you know the time comes for all of us when someone else's biography is not enough?

There comes a time in life when all of us have to write an autobiography. We can't take as our models the sensuous persons of the world, and there is a sense in which we can't take as our models the holy among us. **We've got to write our own stories.**

I think I want to push that a bit because I am aware that there is among us all a hunger for heroes. And while we reject those within religious circles who are openly egotistical and materialistic, we have a tendency to hero-worship those among us who are holy people of God. Especially the people

>with charisma
>>the people in religious "show-biz"
>>>people whose lives are a bit different
>>maybe a little more radical
>or spectacular than ours.

So-and-so had all the money, fame and fortune and he left it all to be a great blessing to the world. Or so-and-so could have been a great opera star but instead is serving Jesus.

If we aren't careful, we can be the spiritual infants Paul talks about in Ephesians: "pushed to and fro, carried about by every wind of doctrine," so that when people with charisma come along and draw us here and draw us there

> we run here
> we run there
> we follow this one
> we follow that one.

Of course, we need examples, but we do not need hero worship! So often in our hero-worship moods and feelings, there is fantasy identification with people who are doing great things for God:

> leaving this
>> doing that
>>> serving here
>>> serving there

and our fantasy identification with them can lead us to the feeling that we have almost done it ourselves, or wish we could have.

We can almost think that we are the ones who are giving, we are the ones who are talented. A fantasy identification with those we hero-worship makes our normal living seem very dull. That kind of thinking and feeling is destructive and useless because we already have a Hero, **Jesus.**

If I understand the Book of Hebrews, it tells us about our Hero, who came right down into the arena

who conquered the foe

who led captivity captive

who gathers us together as His crowd of ragtags

and misfits

and ordinary folk

who become the conquering people of God.

So what we need to do is keep our eyes on Jesus **and begin to write our autobiography!**

I think our immaturity really ends when on the one hand, we turn away from those whose lifestyles are contradictory to what we know of the gospel and example of Jesus, but when we also reverently turn away from those within the community of faith whose unusual lives we admire so much.

Then we begin to build **our own** relationship with God and begin to write our spiritual autobiography. The time will come when we will have to face the issue, **"as for you."**

You know, Timothy couldn't always be a Paul person. Timothy had to be a Timothy person. He had to be a Timothy-Jesus person. He had to be a Jesus-Bible-Timothy person. And he couldn't always live as the disciple of Paul; he had to be his own Jesus-person!

There are those who are living selfish lives. And there are those, like Paul, living holy lives. "But as for you," as for us, we have got to be ourselves and live in Christ.

But we have more resources than our own. Paul says to Timothy, "Continue in what you have learned." And the Sacred Scriptures will lead us to faith in Christ and to maturity in our discipleship.

> [14] But as for you, continue in what you have learned and have firmly believed, knowing from whom you learned it [15] and how from childhood you have been acquainted with the sacred writings which are able to instruct you for salvation through faith in Christ Jesus. [16] All scripture is inspired by God and[a] profitable for teaching, for reproof, for correction, and for training in righteousness, [17] that the man of God may be complete, equipped for every good work. (2 Timothy 3:14-17).

Again and again, we are called back to Christ and back to the Scriptures for the source of our life in Him. I really have been seeing that over and over. And it seems to me in this beautiful passage Paul tells us that fundamentally the Scriptures have two purposes.

One: **the Scriptures bring us to Christ.**

You know the reason New Testament Christians have the Old Testament is because they believe that the Old Testament is really the cradle of Christ. It is the bearer, the bringer of Christ to us. And as we read the Scriptures, **they bring us to Jesus!**

That's why we don't worship the Bible, we worship the Christ to whom the Bible bears witness. The inspired Word of God will lead us to faith in Christ. *I believe that!*

Do you know people who found the Lord without any help just by reading the Bible? I haven't met very many but I have met a few and it's been exciting. **The inspired Word of God will lead us to faith in Christ!**

I have to tell you this, like Timothy I'm third-generation and I know from whom I received it, but I have really come to know Jesus as I have lived and loved and tried to memorize some of His words. I'm sure that's your testimony too.

Two: Paul tells us, as he told Timothy, that **the inspired Scriptures are profitable to lead us to maturity in our discipleship.**

Do you see the two areas: teaching and correction, discipline and instruction in righteousness? The words for teaching and correction used in the original Greek relate to our thought life—actually, our theology. It is interesting that our teaching and correction are both positive and negative. I want to tell you just as simply as I can that what we believe
> about God
> about Christ
> about the ministry of the Holy Spirit
needs to be brought to the Word to let the Word be the controlling element in our understanding.

You know and so do I that we carry around some strange ideas about God. I've lived long enough to believe that some of you have thoughts and ideas about God that are just terrible. They are wrong! I wonder why we don't give them up? Why don't we bring them to Scripture and let the Word of God teach us?

I think in my own journey what has meant more to me than anything else is the understanding that **God is like Jesus.**

I learned that while trying to work my way through John 14, 15, and 16. And when Jesus says, "He who has seen me has seen the Father" (14:9b), do I really believe that?

> In the beginning was the Word, and the Word was with God, and the Word was God. ²He was in the beginning with God; ³all things were made through him, and without him was not anything made that was made. (John 1:1-3). And the word became flesh and dwelt among us (John 1:14).

You see, if I really believe that, it brings two things: it brings correction to my false ideas and teaches me the truth about God and about Christ. That's what the Bible does!

It also brings instruction in righteousness: it tells me how to live and it tells me what to believe.

There is a negative and a positive here too. *Maybe I should testify at this point.* I've discovered in my own life that as I begin to take the Bible seriously it has a way of working down into the behavior patterns of my living.

I don't think I knew what it meant to be a loving person until I started working in First John. *It can be very distressing!* If you take it seriously, old ideas have to crumble. We have to bow down to what we read and what we understand.

I've had the privilege of teaching from the Prophets, *and if you don't want to be messed up, stay out of the Prophets!* In today's society, we've got ourselves in a situation where we can legitimize the differences. We can live in affluence while all around us are people who are hurting and hungry. And so we glibly say, "The poor you have with you always," and go on our way in affluent rejoicing. *Well, if you want to keep that up, stay out of Amos, and stay out of Hosea!*

I don't mind referring to the Old Testament because the Old Testament was all Timothy had, and Paul said the Holy Scriptures are inspired of God
and are profitable. I have found my own life
>   drawn under judgment
>   confronted
>   challenged
>   and brought into new repentance
>   and insight
just because I read these books! **It is profitable for reproof, for correction and for instruction in righteousness!**

I've also been thinking a lot these days about the words of Jesus and asking if we take them seriously. I've been reading and rereading the Sermon on the Mount and I think if I have any good advice for you it is: if you want to live complacently, and drift along, stay out of Matthew 5, 6, 7! *It will mess you up!*

For that matter stay out of Ephesians 4, 5, 6 and Romans 12. *Those passages will change you if you aren't careful!* Keep your guard up because if you get to reading the Bible, you will find it is profitable to bring about change in your life! In fact, the older I get and the more I read the Bible, the more I believe it is inspired! We need to keep
>   reading it
>   praying it
>   thinking it
and saying: "Lord what do You want to say to me. What needs to happen in me?"

And when I do that, I see things that are
> disturbing
> and helpful
> and instructive

and again, I realize **it is an inspired Book!** If we will come under it, it will speak to us with authority and change our lives!

What I am trying to say to you is that if we will bow down to Scripture and seek to release our
> preconceived ideas
> and prejudices
> and bring ourselves under its authority

it becomes a life-changing power in our lives!

Let's go back to when Jesus began to write His autobiography. There in the wilderness of His temptation, the way He used Scripture was tremendously important. Both Jesus and the devil used Scripture!

What made the Scripture authoritative in the life of Jesus and destructive in the mouth of Satan? Is Scripture any less Scripture because the devil quotes it? You know the Bible is the Bible is the Bible and the devil can quote the Bible. What is it that makes it the inspired Word, the authoritative Word? I'll tell you what it is. **Satan used it but Jesus obeyed it and lived it!**

Satan said, "Command these stones to become loaves of bread" (Matthew 4:3). Jesus said, "Man shall not live by bread alone, but by every word that proceeds from the mouth of God" (Matthew 4:4). We know that Jesus did that. He didn't live by bread alone. He'd been fasting already. He lived by what came from His Father.

Satan said to Him, "Throw yourself down; for it is written he will give his angels charge of you" (Matthew 4:5). And Jesus' response of Scripture was, "You shall not tempt the Lord your God" (Matthew 4:7).

So the devil uses Scripture and Jesus uses Scripture. That's not just playing with the Sword of the Spirit, that's not scriptural sword playing. It is for real!

Don't try to out-memorize, out proof-text others. That's misusing the Word of God! Jesus did not ever tempt God His Father, and He went all the way from the Mount of Temptation down to the valley and all the way to Calvary and **NEVER PUT HIS FATHER TO THE TEST!** In His time of testing, Jesus submitted every desire and every inclination to the Word and the will of His Father and obeyed the verdict that He found there.

You know, I get scared when people say: "OK, God, You gotta do this and that. You've gotta come through." Don't do that. **Never!** You can never back God into a corner!

No, Jesus lived in
    obedience
        and faith
           and trust
           when the crowd was against Him
        when everything was beautiful
      when everything was ugly.
All the way even to the point of experiencing ultimate and personal alienation, He lived by the Word and didn't tempt His Father!

Well, that's the way it is with us too. "You shall worship the Lord your God and him only shall you serve" (Matthew 4:10).

Here's the point: in the circle of religious folk there is a variety of
    behavior
        lifestyles and
            value structures
that are contradictory to what we know of Jesus and His example.
But, praise God in this religious circle there are God's
            gracious
        good
      godly
    holy people.
But then comes the Word **"As for you, continue in what you have learned."**

As we seek to write our autobiographies, we have the gracious, inspired Word of God that brings us to Jesus and brings us to the Truth.

We're going to get our words to live by from somewhere. **Jesus got His from His Father**. Thank God that through His Spirit, we have His Word today! Let's pray.

Father, we thank Thee that as we begin to face our own lives and build our own authentic relationship with Thee, and grow in our own discipleship, there is the example of godly persons and there is the Word of God that brings us to Jesus. And the Word of God is profitable to teach us what we need to know about how we need to live. So, give us grace to bow down to it, and to Thee. In Thy name and for Thy glory. Amen.

6
Where We Get Our Model
2 Timothy 2:8-13

In these last moments I would like to share with you in general what
God has been saying to me from Second Timothy. I have been
  reading
  and rereading
  and thinking
  and praying about this book
and I must say that it has strengthened some convictions that have
been growing in me.

I think you already know that I do not come to you out of a
vacuum—out of nowhere.
    I have a context.
    I am on my journey.
    I live in a real world
    with real people
    and have real needs
    and I don't have many answers.

But some things have been working in my life of late and I have had them strengthened as I have read Second Timothy. I want to go back to the first chapter and read it again with you:

> [8] Do not be ashamed then of testifying to our Lord, nor of me his prisoner, but share in suffering for the gospel in the power of God, [9] who saved us and called us with a holy calling, not in virtue of our works but in virtue of his own purpose and the grace which he gave us in Christ Jesus ages ago, [10] and now has manifested through the appearing of our Savior Christ Jesus, who abolished death and brought life and immortality to light through the gospel. [11] For this gospel I was appointed a preacher and apostle and teacher, [12] and therefore I suffer as I do. But I am not ashamed, for I know whom I have believed, and I am sure that he is able to guard until that Day what has been entrusted to me.[a] [13] Follow the pattern of the sound words which you have heard from me, in the faith and love which are in Christ Jesus; [14] guard the truth that has been entrusted to you by the Holy Spirit who dwells within us. (2 Timothy 1:8-14)

The concepts that I found in Second Timothy,
    the language
        metaphors
            unspoken value systems
seem to me to stand clearly and definitely against the
                value systems
         ideals
      models and
    goals of our world.

I have seen in a new way that
    the ideal for the Kingdom

the value structure

the goals that we are to have in the kingdom of God
are out of harmony with those in the world around us.

We read over and over again in this little epistle words like
suffering
persecution
hold steady
be firm.

Then, at the close of the old apostle's life he mentions in chapter four:
"I have fought the good fight, I have finished the race, I have kept
the faith."

There **is** a fight to be fought.
There **is** a race to be run.
There **is** a faith to be kept.

It is very clear to me that the
ideals
the goals
the values
the meaningful things
that are ours in the Kingdom
are different from those in the world!

I have come to realize that it is pretty easy for us in the church to get
our models from our present systems and to let ourselves be molded
by current
values
goals and
ideals from the culture around us.
I believe that!

And so we have the success models. The church as a corporate
institution takes its place in the community. It is supposed to be a good
place to live so if you want to buy good real estate you buy it close to
>a school
>>a church
>>>a shopping center
>>playgrounds
and everything else that contributes to good living.

It is difficult
>**not** to fall into the success patterns
>**not** to assume the corporate image
>**not** to take our place in upward mobility
>**not** to judge ourselves by the success ideals of the world.

It's hard not to do that because we are an institution. Churches are
institutions and we want success. And so, if we are not careful, we
model our churches, after the corporate image and ourselves after
the corporate executive, and do what we have to do to be successful.
And with all our faults we are the nicest people we know!

Do you know what the expectation is?
>That the young will fall in line
>>and will be successful
>>>and handsome
>>>>and beautiful
>>>>>and talented
>>>>>>and educated
>>>>>and will move on in a few years
>>>>to take places of leadership
>>>in our fine churches

in our fine communities
in our fine corporations and institutions of our fine country.

And so, we move up and out and become
more affluent
and more successful
and walk into all the levels of society
and all the phony value structures.

And then I see Jesus come
and walk into all the levels of our society
and interrupt all of the false and phony value
structures
and kneel down
and wash disciples' feet.

And I hear Paul's words to Timothy when he said, "Follow the
pattern of sound words which you have heard from me." Don't move
away from the tradition of the gospel that has
abolished death
stirred faith
introduced immortality
and which has been manifested in the life
and teaching
and death
and resurrection
of Jesus.

So, as we look for our models
of discipleship
and behavior
for living

we've got a place to look and a Person to look to!

I come under judgment too and I am distressed because I am
hearing what God is saying.

    I have a nice home.

    I have a nice family.

    I have a nice place of ministry.

I know what it means to be part of an educational institution of the
church. I know what the "good life" is.

    It involves clothes that cost more

        but aren't worth the labels.

    It involves cars and houses and lifestyles

        to protect the correct success image.

I realize we can partake of the fallenness of our fallen world if we

    build our structures

        get our images, ideals, and goals

            from the world around us.

Do you see the tension and stress that exists?!

    I **do** live in this world.

    I **do** need a car to get to work.

    I **do** need a house to live in.

    I **do** need affirmation.

    I **do** need some things

and so do we all!

But if they never come under the judgment of God

    if they never bow down to the life and teaching of Jesus

        if it comes about that we develop success patterns

            and move up

and out of patterns that are in harmony
with the life and teaching of Jesus
then it is time to repent. I guess it is time for me to repent too!

Here we are together. We live in this world
with its sensualism
and materialism
and the success models that influence us.

And I hear the words of Phillips's paraphrase of Romans 12:2,
"Don't let the world around you squeeze you into its own mould."

But sometimes I fear that the church exerts a considerable amount of
pressure. The pressure is on us
to succeed
to do the best
to reflect the "bigger is better" syndrome
to move up and out.
*And, of course, we'll double our tithe and get rich. That's not really true,
you know.*

I hear from Second Timothy that the pressures and lifestyles of
Timothy's world are not unlike the pressures and lifestyles of the
world in which we now live with its sophisticated and complicated
success formulas.

And I hear the call
to keep true to the gospel
to hold fast to the tradition
which is the passing on of the life
and teaching
and death

and resurrection
of Jesus Christ our Lord.

Well, thank God!

What we can know for sure is
the One who took the lowly path to Calvary's cross
who lived the life of servanthood
who taught us to love our enemies as well as each other
who challenged us to build our lives in accordance with His
who called us to take up our cross and follow Him—
THAT MAN DIED ON THE CROSS AND GOD RAISED HIM
FROM THE DEAD! **HE BECOMES OUR BASIS FOR HOPE,
MEANING, AND INTEGRITY!**

As we go, we go to
live at the Cross
in the power of the Resurrection
and in the fellowship and communion
of the Holy Spirit.
Praise God!

I don't know what your
dreams
goals
desires
are but we must keep our value systems at the Cross and remember
who it is we are following!
He is the Man who loved the poor
and washed the disciples' feet
and went to Calvary's cross to die.

He is the one who is our Lord and Master!